“Konarzewska succeeds in interpreting the most famous texts of Gombrowicz and, by linking them with European cultural history, lifting the mask of this literary chameleon and his hidden gay life. A good read for anyone who enjoys the subversion of the national and has a penchant for the grotesque.”

Alexander Wöll, *Chair of Culture and Literature of Central and Eastern Europe, University of Potsdam, Germany*

Gombrowicz

This book is a short introduction to Witold Gombrowicz's life and work as one of the most prominent figures in twentieth-century literature and theater, providing intertextual perspectives that allow readers to analyze his short stories, plays, and novels in broad contexts.

Gombrowicz (1904–1969) was a writer and philosopher whose experimental literary works belong to the stream of European existentialism and simultaneously mark the birth of postmodernism. In Gombrowicz's grotesque universe, there is no separation between literature, biography, sexuality, and philosophy. His novels, including *Ferdydurke, Trans-Atlantyk,* and *Pornography*, contain autobiographical elements, whereas in his renowned *Diary*, daily life becomes an object of sophisticated philosophical reflection that links introspection with humor and a gift for observation.

Gombrowicz: An Introduction is an approachable guide for students and instructors of Slavic literature and culture, comparative literature, philosophy, and theater studies.

Aleksandra Konarzewska works in the Institute of Slavic Languages and Literatures at the University of Tübingen, Germany. She is a literary scholar and historian of ideas of Eastern and Central Europe.

Routledge Histories of Central and Eastern Europe

The nations of Central and Eastern Europe experienced a time of momentous change in the period following the Second World War. The vast majority were subject to Communism and central planning while events such as the Hungarian uprising and Prague Spring stood out as key watershed moments against a distinct social, cultural and political backcloth. With the fall of the Berlin Wall, German reunification and the break-up of the Soviet Union, changes from the 1990s onwards have also been momentous with countries adjusting to various capitalist realities. The volumes in this series will help shine a light on the experiences of this key geopolitical zone with many lessons to be learned for the future.

The Rise and Fall of Communist Yugoslavism
Soft Nation-Building in Yugoslavia
Tomaž Ivešić

The Eastern Bloc and Sub-Saharan Africa
Czechoslovakia, UNESCO and Development Aid from the 1960s and beyond
Barbora Buzássyová

Time and Material Culture
Rethinking Soviet Temporalities
Edited by Julie Deschepper, Antony Kalashnikov, and Federica Rossi

Gombrowicz
An Introduction
Aleksandra Konarzewska

For more information about this series, please visit: https://www.routledge.com/Routledge-Histories-of-Central-and-Eastern-Europe/book-series/CEE

Gombrowicz

An Introduction

Aleksandra Konarzewska

LONDON AND NEW YORK

First published 2024
by Routledge
4 Park Square, Milton Park, Abingdon, Oxon OX14 4RN

and by Routledge
605 Third Avenue, New York, NY 10158

Routledge is an imprint of the Taylor & Francis Group, an informa business

Funded by the Federal Ministry of Education and Research (BMBF) and the Baden-Württemberg Ministry of Science as part of the Excellence Strategy of the German Federal and State Governments ("Program for the Promotion of Junior Researchers," grant number: PRO-KONARZ-2022-8).

British Library Cataloguing-in-Publication Data
A catalogue record for this book is available from the British Library

ISBN: 978-1-032-01043-4 (hbk)
ISBN: 978-1-032-02575-9 (pbk)
ISBN: 978-1-003-18397-6 (ebk)

DOI: 10.4324/9781003183976

Typeset in Times New Roman
by KnowledgeWorks Global Ltd.

Contents

Acknowledgments

Witold Gombrowicz's literary world is a complex one, as is known by everyone who has read (or tried to read) his *Ferdydurke*, *The Marriage*, or *Operetta*. The main idea of the following book was thus to offer an auxiliary tool that might help those readers of Gombrowicz's prose and plays who might feel uncertain when exposed for the first time to the orgiastic, baroque language of his *Trans-Atlantyk* or the cold grotesque of the short stories *Bacacay*. I remember my first uneasy contact with the literary universe of Gombrowicz and how much time I needed to fully immerse myself in his humor, audacious imagination, and sensitivity, and at the same time to realize the size of his enormous intellectual rigidness and independence. Hence, if *Gombrowicz: An Introduction* helps its readers enjoy Gombrowicz's work a little more, its main aim will have been accomplished.

It takes a village to raise a child; it takes a number of people to make a book. First and foremost, I am grateful to the Routledge publishing house and my editors, Robert Langham and Kaustav Ghosh, for their willingness to engage in this project and their belief that such an *Introduction* will fill a certain gap in the gombrowiczologist book market. Without their consideration, support, and patience, the following book would have never been completed. My outstanding student assistants, Julia Furmańczyk and Zuzanna Tymoftyjewicz (University of Tübingen), made the first readings of each chapter and took care of the final shape of the bibliography and references. Finally, John Heath helped me infinitely with the copyediting of the book.

Working on Gombrowicz allows us to gain a better understanding of the middle-age phrase about "dwarfs standing on the shoulders of giants." Without the persistent, meticulous, and diligent work of editors, researchers, publishers, and endorsers, many of whom have spent decades scrupulously editing Gombrowicz's works, ensuring their accessibility and contextualizing his oeuvre for academic and non-academic audiences (e.g., by collecting the testimonies and memoirs), this book could have never been written. Without such people as Jan Błoński, Włodzimierz Bolecki, Jerzy Giedroyc, Rita Gombrowicz, Andrzej S. Kowalczyk, Jerzy Jarzębski, Joanna Siedlecka, and Klementyna Suchanow, gombrowiczology in today's form would not exist. By the same token, I am grateful to generations of scholars, commentators, writers, and readers whose analyses have shaped the ways we think about Gombrowicz's prose and drama today. Some of them kindly agreed to share their thoughts on the following book. I wish to thank Silvia Dapía (City University of New York), Ewa Kobyłecka-Piwońska (University of Łódź, Poland), and Silvana Mandolessi (KU Leuven), who read and commented on fragments on Gombrowicz's life and work in Argentina, pointing out many important details. Polish history is complex, and hence I am also deeply thankful to Michał Przeperski (Polish Academy of Science) and Karolina Kołpak (Yale University), who went through the second chapter of the book and drew my attention to some aspects of Central European history in the first half of the twentieth century.

Some other parts of the book were also read and discussed by the participants in the Slavic literary colloquia in the first half of 2022, organized as joint events by scholars from Fribourg, Bern, and Basel (Switzerland) and (online) by researchers from Tübingen, Würzburg, and Münster (Germany). I am grateful not only for their constructive and helpful feedback but also for their genuine encouragement and enthusiasm for the project. I wish to thank Thomas Grob, Anna Hodel Laszlo, Gunnar Lenz (University of Basel), Karina Bukiewicz, Eliane Fitze, Patrick Flack, Jens Herlth, Andrey Kozlov, Aleksandra Sikorska, Christian Zehnder (University of Fribourg), Daniela Amodio, Elena Glöcker, Valentin Peshanskyi, Irina Wutsdorff (University of Münster), Gesine Drews-Sylla (University of Würzburg), in addition to Natalia Borisova, Jennifer Döring, Julia Furmańczyk, and Schamma Schahadat (University of Tübingen). Many ideas for the book also resulted from the discussions with Tübingen students who attended my monographic seminars on Witold Gombrowicz from 2020 to 2022 and whose fresh, unbiased perspectives helped me see many aspects of his work in a new light (for instance, I would never have thought of the Minister in *Trans-Atlantyk* as of someone who is "just doing his job, and in quite difficult circumstances").

The larger part of the book was written in Switzerland, where I spent a year at the University of Fribourg as part of the Swiss Government Excellence Scholarship. There, despite the COVID-19 pandemic and many related inconveniences, I enjoyed genuine hospitability, perfect working conditions, and thorough institutional support. My gratitude goes to Sandra Nast from the International Relation Office and Jens Herlth, the head of the Institute of Slavic Studies, whose flexibility, willingness to help, and savvy enabled solutions to every bureaucratic difficulty related to my stay. Some of the publications costs were covered by the German Federal Ministry of Education and Research (BMBF) and the Baden-Württemberg Ministry of Science as part of the Excellence Strategy of the German Federal and State Governments ("Program for the Promotion of Junior Researchers," grant number: PRO-KONARZ-2022-8). I would like to thank Dr. Sonja Großmann from Department II. 2 (Research Support) at the University of Tübingen for her guidance and help with the research schedule and financial planning.

In Fribourg, during the conference *Social Imagination: Relations Between Social Sciences and Polish Literature 1880–1939*, organized by Jens Herlth and Aleksandra Sikorska in June 2022, I held a talk on Gombrowicz's pre-war oeuvre. In September 2022, I participated in the conference *Time Out of Joint: Literary (Re)Visions of Time in Eastern and Central Europe*, organized by Alexander Wöll, Bohdan Tokarskyi, and Eugen Rube at the University of Potsdam (Germany), and was given the opportunity to present several ideas that appear in *Diary*, *Ferdydurke*, and *Trans-Atlantyk* and to reconsider them from the perspective of the dramatic year of 2022. I wish to thank the organizers of both events for the awe-inspiring time and the further possibility to rethink and re-discuss the topicality of Gombrowicz's work today.

Last but not least, I would like to thank my dear K., who is the best friend, supporter, and conversation partner ever, and who, I hope, will have no excuse but to finally read Gombrowicz's *Ferdydurke*.

Munich, summer 2023

Abbreviations

BAC Witold Gombrowicz, *Bacacay*, trans. Bill Johnston (New York: Archipelago Books, 2006)

COS Witold Gombrowicz, *Cosmos*, trans. Danuta Borchardt (New Haven: Yale University Press, 1900)

D Witold Gombrowicz, *Diary*, trans. Lillian Vallee (New Haven: Yale University Press, 2012)

FER Witold Gombrowicz, *Ferdydurke*, trans. Danuta Borchardt (New Haven, London: Yale University Press, 2000)

GP Witold Gombrowicz, *A Guide to Philosophy in Six Hours and Fifteen Minutes*, trans. Benjamin Ivry (New Haven: Yale University Press, 2004

PLA Witold Gombrowicz, *Three Plays: Princess Ivona, The Marriage, Operetta*, trans. Krystyna Griffith-Jones, Catherine Robins, Louis Iribarne (London, New York: Marion Boyars, 1998)

PM Witold Gombrowicz, *Polish Memories*, trans. Bill Johnston (New Haven, London: Yale University Press, 2011)

POR Witold Gombrowicz, *Pornografia. A Novel*, trans. Danuta Borchardt (New York: Grove Press, 2009)

T-A Witold Gombrowicz, *Trans-Atlantyk*, trans. Nina Karsov and Carolyn French (New Haven, London: Yale University Press, 1994)

TES Witold Gombrowicz, *A Kind of Testament*, with assistance of Dominique de Roux, trans. Alasdair Hamilton (Champaign, Ill.: Dalkey Archive Press, 2007)

1 Introduction

Figure 1.1 Witold Gombrowicz in Vence. Author: Bohdan Paczowski. Public Domain. Gombrowicz spent his last years in Vence, France, where he continued his creative work.

It would be no exaggeration to state that the Polish-Argentinian writer Witold Marian Gombrowicz (1904–1969) is one of the most prominent figures in twentieth-century literature and theater. In his works, one finds creative and inspiring dialogue with the crucial intellectual streams of his time (particularly existentialism), as his entire literary oeuvre permeates the rumination on the artificiality and arbitrariness of different norms (social, aesthetical, and discursive), while simultaneously acknowledging them as an almost

DOI: 10.4324/9781003183976-1

metaphysical inevitability. This alone would allow readers to place him in the ranks of such authors as Bruno Schulz, Albert Camus, Milan Kundera, Jean-Paul Sartre, and Samuel Beckett. What makes Gombrowicz's work exceptional is his masterful command of combining the local with the universal, the lower with the higher, the national with the global, the sensual with the sensible, the trivial with the deep, the traditional with the modern, and the grotesque with the serious in his own, incomparably vivid, entertaining, and brilliant way.

Gombrowicz fashioned his literary realms from the world he personally observed and experienced; he was undoubtedly not an author who would confine himself to a library, conducting extensive research to craft a compelling historical novel. He was born in 1904 into a family of Polish landed gentry in Małoszyce, which was then part of the Russian Empire, and spent his formative years in Warsaw, Poland, where he completed his studies at the Faculty of Law and made his literary debut. His experimental novel *Ferdydurke* (1937) first brought him recognition within the Polish literary spheres. At the moment of the outbreak of the Second World War, Gombrowicz found himself in Buenos Aires, Argentina, where he resided for almost a quarter of a century. Despite encountering numerous challenges as an exiled author writing in a Slavic language, Gombrowicz persevered as an active writer, making a significant contribution to the international recognition of Polish literature and in many aspects even surpassing the appreciation of other esteemed Polish novelists and poets of his time, including Zbigniew Herbert, Stanisław Lem, or Czesław Miłosz. Gombrowicz was the first Polish author of the twentieth century whose works, despite being written in the middle of the Cold War era, creatively challenged the East–West axis, introducing instead an axis (or, more precisely, a link) between North and South.[1] Interestingly, the protagonists of Gombrowicz's literary works almost always consist of the Polish and Argentinian middle class, intelligentsia, and rural gentry[2]; whether it was the atmosphere of a pretentious bed and breakfast in Zakopane during the 1930s or the bustling ambiance of a café in Buenos Aires during the 1950s, Gombrowicz relied on his own sensibilities, taste, and discernment to bring his narratives, essays, and semi-autobiographical writings to life.

Intellectual self-reliance is perhaps one of the keys to Gombrowicz's oeuvre. Taking into account that he was socialized in a culture that for historical reasons promoted different ideals, such as group solidarity and loyalty, this aspect of his work is hard to underestimate. Gombrowicz's life was not easy; nor was the epoch in which he lived. Yet in his oeuvre, he relentlessly follows the conviction that resignation from honest self-introspection in the name of respecting someone's difficult situation or hurt feelings is intellectual blackmail and that maturity requires being true to yourself, even if it involves being unpleasant or impudent.[3] His long-life master was Thomas Mann (1875–1955),[4] and the motto he followed was the classical modernist approach to art and the artist presented in Mann's short story "Tonio Kröger" (1903), where the eponymous protagonist expresses the belief that genuine artists and writers must maintain a detached and aloof stance toward human emotions and experiences, viewing them as banal and futile, and suggesting that the writer's creative power lies in their cool and fastidious attitude, as well as in their ability to distance themselves from the depths of human sentiment.[5] In his *Diary* and *Testament*, Gombrowicz follows this thought and openly questions the naïve belief that being a victim of historical circumstances such as political persecution automatically makes one morally superior or more insightful (in his native Poland, such a conviction has very deep and strong roots). As he coldly observes, "[n]o historical steamroller will squeeze important words out of an immature people" (D 71), as "important words" require not suffering but intellectual effort. Piotr Sadzik points out that in Gombrowicz's worldview, every value (ethical or aesthetical) must be dialectically challenged by its opposite; otherwise, there is a risk that one will quickly start to reproduce platitudes—"and these," Sadzik says, "even if they are right, turn us into repeaters who give up their subjectivity."[6] In such a perspective, Gombrowicz is not a promoter of ideological escapism or conformist indifferentism, but rather someone who subtly warns from unreflective affections and automatic performing the gestures that are ascribed to a given group identity.[7]

Nonetheless, even though Gombrowicz's oeuvre caustically disdains the easy relief that comes with sharing the dominant mindset of one's community or social group (class, nation, and gender), many of his works at the same time do provide a healthy dose of anarchistic, cathartic humor. In Poland, his novels are conceived to this day as a breath of fresh air in a dusty room. Hence, even if claims that Gombrowicz's works are "as central in Polish culture as [Adam] Mickiewicz's have been from the early nineteenth century onward"[8] might seem exaggerated, it is indeed hard to deny that many characteristics of his work–distance toward group sentiment (particularly the nation), self-irony that allows one to laugh at oneself, and a common-sense skepticism and nonchalance toward any intellectual fashion, be it conservative or progressive—are present in the postwar Polish culture to a vast extent thanks to him and his literary impertinences. The influence of Gombrowicz is visible due to the fact that in the contemporary, rapidly secularizing and libertarianizing Poland,[9] much of his worldview (e.g., his ironical approach to the patriotic pompousness) has become a regular cultural code found not only in literary works but also in songs, comic novels, memes, and films. It is also hard to imagine the work of renowned present-day authors (Olga Tokarczuk, Andrzej Sapkowski, Jacek Dukaj, Szczepan Twardoch, Ziemowit Szczerek) without the path set by such literary gems as *Ferdydurke* or *Trans-Atlantyk*.[10]

At the same time, Gombrowicz's writing exhibits several characteristics that might make it challenging for readers. The first one is emotional frigidity. In words of the Polish writer Czesław Miłosz, Gombrowicz's literary work is characterized by a "cold" and "atheist" quality and a calm focus on the complexities of human nature rather than the appreciation of the allure of the world.[11] The second are Gombrowicz's formal experiments with language, manipulating syntax, capitalizing random words for effect, and blending idiolects. The clearest example is the experimental novella *Trans-Antlantyk* (1953), which begins in the following way:

> I feel a need to relate here for Family, kin and friends of mine the beginning of these my adventures, now ten years old, in the Argentinian capital. Not that I ask anyone to have these old Noodles of mine, this Turnip (haply even raw), for in the Pewter bowl Thin, Wretched they are and, what is more, likewise Shaming, in the oil of my Sins, my Shames, these Groats of mine, heavy, Dark with this black kasha of mine—oh, better not to heave it to the Mouth save for eternal Curse, for my Humiliation, on the perennial track of my Life and up that hard, wearisome Mountain of mine.
>
> (T-A 3)

Despite distancing himself from the *nouveau roman* literary movement,[12] some of Gombrowicz's works, such as his latest novel *Cosmos* (1965), demonstrate influences from this style.[13] Michał P. Markowski describes Gombrowicz as an "anti-narrativist," similar to Georges Perec (1936–1982), as they often begin anew and resist traditional narrative progression, resulting in novels that lack classical endings.[14] Janusz Margański adds that in Gombrowicz's works, there is barely any deeper understanding between the protagonists, as their communication is of a phatic nature, which means that individual utterances serve merely as a ritual of small talk and are thus devoid of any causal power.[15]

*

The following book is organized into five chapters, each focusing on a different significant motif of Gombrowicz's literary oeuvre. As it is meant to be of an introductory and general character, I focus on Gombrowicz's canonical literary works: stories from the volume *Bacacay*, the novels *Ferdydurke*, *Pornografia*, *Trans-Atlantyk*, *Cosmos*, three plays. Since they are sufficiently dense and challenging (due to both their experimental form and the actual content), I decided to concentrate on them, even if it required putting aside the novel in episodes *Possessed* (*Opętani*, 1939), short stories, minor philosophical works, reportages, essays, and pieces of literary criticism, as well as Gombrowicz's private notes, *Kronos*, published as a book in 2013.[16] For the same reason, I provide no original quotations in Polish or Spanish, but rely on the extant English translations. (Where that is not the case, my own translations are marked as such).

Gombrowicz: An Introduction begins by discussing the question of violence and cruelty, understood in a multifaceted sense, as in his works, Gombrowicz depicts social norms, relations within families, systems of youth socialization (particularly at schools), and relationships toward people and animals as violent and absurdly cruel. His early prose, the collection of short stories *Recollections from Adolescence* (1933; renamed *Bacacay* in 1957), and the experimental novel *Ferdydurke* (1937) reflect the intense yet grim years between the two world wars: the feeling of insecurity after the disappearance of the European "old world" in 1918, the rise of fascism, anti-Semitism, poverty, contempt, and the merciless exploitation of the lower classes. In his later works, particularly in *Diary*, *Pornografia*, and *Cosmos*, Gombrowicz's way of presenting violence is more subtle and quiet, but the question of deliberate cruelty (especially toward animals) nonetheless becomes much more visible and critical.

The second crucial topic of Gombrowicz's literary universe is eroticism. Even though, as Ewa Thompson notes, this universe is "a loveless world,"[17] the question of human sexuality is one of the most important motifs in Gombrowicz's works and is present in his oeuvre from the very beginning. Paradoxically, it is usually not "the higher" but "the lower" (the ugly, the dirty, the nasty) that is more appealing. In his early short prewar stories and in the novel *Ferdydurke*, there appear motifs of various erotic fixations and fetishes, such as an obsession with the stranger (the short story "Lawyer Kraykowski's Dancer") and an erotic fascination with a farmhand (*parobek*), or with unattractive lower-class women (*Ferdydurke*; short story "On the Kitchen Steps"). In almost all cases, erotic drives are presented calmly and not without caustic sarcasm (as in the short story "Virginity"), as if the main aim were an analytical exploration of certain mechanisms that are the cause of sexual interests. In his later works, particularly in *Trans-Atlantyk*, *Pornografia*, and *Diary*, Gombrowicz depicts erotic interactions in an entirely different way: despite the vibe of absurdity and lovelessness, sexual passions cease to be reduced to objects of an unruffled analysis only, and the sphere of eroticism becomes enriched with a relaxed merriment and delight. Moreover, sexual attraction comes to be unironically related to the youth and the beauty of a young body: it is solely age that decides whether someone can be sexually appetizing or not; eroticism thus leads to the realization of one's own transience and finitude. Gombrowicz's last works, *Operetta* and *Cosmos*, link eroticism with the existential question of nothingness.

The next chapter focuses on how Gombrowicz's oeuvres challenge readers to see the question of human identity in a new light. Gombrowicz belonged to those intellectuals of the twentieth century who were deeply suspicious of any group loyalties that could result from established identity categories, such as nation, gender, race, ethnicity, or class. (In the first half of the twentieth century in Europe, particularly ethnic and national identity could decide life or death). As a Polish-Argentinian writer and thinker, Gombrowicz was acutely aware of the moral and aesthetic dilemmas of one's own belonging to a semi-peripheral cultural community and sought to explore the fraught relationship between individual identity and the collective identity of a nation, discerningly reflecting the ways In which inhabitants of the "countries of degraded

Form" (to use his own phrase, TES 66) must negotiate their place in the world. Particularly in his monumental *Diary* (1953–1969), he formulates numerous objections to treating historical collective traumata as an excuse for one's own immature behavior (and in the case of artists and intellectuals, for producing banal and uninteresting works). In Gombrowicz's eyes, each individual is responsible for their intellectual development and should strive to uphold their own standards of sincerity, spiritual independence, human dignity, and good taste, even in the face of difficult circumstances.

Another aspect of the identity question explored by Gombrowicz remains the issue of professional identity among writers and artists in the modern age, especially in light of the postwar massification of culture. This raises the question not only of quality but also of quantity, as humorously presented in the character Gonzalo in *Trans-Atlantyk*, who hires professional readers to keep up with his vast (and constantly growing) collection of books. A recurring theme in Gombrowicz's *Diary* and some minor theoretical works is also the tendency toward excessive intellectualization in cultural discourse and the proliferation of oversophisticated theories and incomprehensible "-isms," which efficiently stifle the creativity of contemporary artists and writers.[18] According to Michał P. Markowski, this allows us to see in Gombrowicz a genuine existentialist—someone who puts "the singular, his very own, the concrete, and the unique in a human being above any concepts, system and science."[19]

Markowski's observation confirms that a further topic intrinsically belonging to Gombrowicz's oeuvre is intersubjectivity, that is, the interactive relationship between individuals and their subjective experiences. Initially introduced by German philosopher Edmund Husserl, who believed that our perception of the world is not solely individual but also influenced by social interactions and the insights of others, intersubjectivity is one of the main concepts developed in the literary works of Albert Camus and Jean-Paul Sartre and is also crucial for understanding one of Gombrowicz's key ideas: Form. Form is not easily changeable like clothing; it is rather a result of ever-changing cultural and social norms, practices, and interactions. Gombrowicz emphasizes in many of his works (*Ferdydurke*, *Trans-Atlantyk*, *Diary*) that one person shapes another, highlighting the interdependence between individuals. The concept of Form is primarily metaphysical rather than political or sociological, as Gombrowicz prioritizes the uncanny and fascinating act of mutual challenges and reshaping of concrete individualities over the cultural, political, and social influences on identity. Those intuitions are particularly visible in Gombrowicz's theater works, which, characterized by absurdity and confrontation, invite audiences to confront the irrationality and interconnectedness of the world. In *Princess Ivona* (1938), his first play, the bare existence of an individual becomes literally dependent on being accepted and liked by others: the main hero is killed only because she is considered to be annoying. The theme of intersubjectivity is further developed in the drama play *The Marriage* (1948, 1953), where Gombrowicz sets the question of the creation of the individual by another individual at a new level and explores the desire for genuine interhuman connections and the interconnectedness of humanity. Gombrowicz's last play, *Operetta* (1966), even though it incorporates the theme of social revolution (portrayed in a grotesque and whimsically peculiar fashion), also emphasizes the profound importance of interpersonal relationships, whereby the desires and behaviors of the characters are influenced by their mutual perceptions of one another.

The final chapter concerns how in Gombrowicz's entire literary work, philosophy occupies a prominent position and purely metaphysical questions serve as a recurring theme. Gombrowicz's somewhat dilettante, yet devoted engagement with philosophy, in most cases expressed in his novels, dramas, and short stories in a subtle, allusive form, extends beyond abstract musings, delving into the realm of human experience, and the complexities of existence. The exploration of existential concepts, particularly the interplay between being and non-being, assumes a significant role, albeit with variations over time. In his early literary works, Gombrowicz engages rather with the notion of being and its different *modi*, for instance within the context of a debate between analytical and synthetical approaches. The tension between parts and the whole, as well as the relationship between elements and the entirety, forms key elements of the philosophical inquiry. As Gombrowicz's writing progresses in time, his focus gradually shifts toward the concept of nothingness, emphasizing the ephemeral and transient nature of human existence. Following the path established in Western philosophy by Arthur Schopenhauer, he situates physical pain (not only among humans but also among other feeling subjects)[20] as a philosophical question that transcends the confines of overly rational ruminations, highlighting its existential significance and evoking a sense of concrete and lived experience.

Notes

1 See: Anita Starosta, *Form and Instability: Eastern Europe, Literature, Postimperial Difference* (Evanston: Northwestern University Press, 2016). As Starosta notices, in that respect, there is a parallel between Gombrowicz and the marvelous Polish nonfiction writer Ryszard Kapuściński (1932–2007).

2 Certain exceptions to that rule are Gombrowicz's drama plays. See Chapter 5.

3 As Tul'si Bhambry notices, "[a]rtistic courage, integrity and self-gratification are key to the public image Gombrowicz forged for himself in the postwar years." Bhambry, Tul'si (Tuesday), "'The Quieter the Louder Indeed': Silence and the Space of Literature in *Trans-Atlantyk*," in *Gombrowicz in Transnational Context: Translation, Affect, and Politics*, ed. Silvia G. Dapía, 154–168 (New York: Routledge, 2019), 157.

4 As Gombrowicz admitted in 1960, "[Thomas Mann] is the only contemporary writer I would like to kiss the hand of. [...] No one knew better how to approach my emotions" (my translation from the German). In: "33 Schriftsteller Nennen Ihre Literarischen Leitbilder," *Tagesblatt* (25.12.1960), GEN MSS 515 Box 16 f. 549, Witold Gombrowicz Archive, Beinecke Rare Book and Manuscript Library, Yale University.

5 Thomas Mann, "Tonio Kröger," in *Frühe Erzählungen 1893–1912: In der Fassung der Großen kommentierten Frankfurter Ausgabe*, 243–318 (Frankfurt am Main: Fischer Taschenbuch Verlag, 2008), 266–283. Cf. Gombrowicz's letter to French author and translator Suzane Arlet in which precisely this fragment of "Tonio Kröger" is invoked as the best description of the relationship between an author, their work, and life. Quoted in: Joanna Siedlecka, *Jaśniepanicz: O Witoldzie Gombrowiczu* (Kraków: Wydawnictwo Literackie, 1987), 272.

6 Joanna Piechura and Piotr Sadzik, "Maranizm pozwala na rewolucyjną i kompleksową rewizję polskiej kultury: [Rozmowa Joanny Piechury z Piotrem Sadzikiem]," *Krytyka Polityczna*, https://krytykapolityczna.pl/kultura/czytaj-dalej/maranizm-w-literaturze-polskiej-rozmowa-joanny-piechury-z-piotrem-sadzikiem/ (accessed April 19, 2023).

7 Ibid.

8 Halina Filipowicz, "Fission and Fusion: Polish Émigré Literature," *Slavic and East European Journal* 33, no. 2 (1989): 162–163.

9 The best example is the systematically rising support for the LGBTQ+ rights, including marriage equality. As the leading Polish NGO "Love Does Not Exclude" Association (Stowarzyszenie "Miłość Nie Wyklucza") points out, citing data from Eurobarometer (from the years 2015 and 2019) and Polish public opinion polling institutions, the number of Poles supporting equal rights for LGBTQ+ people is steadily rising, despite various bigotted and homophobic governmental agendas and initiatives. According to IPSOS polls in 2021, 56 percent of respondents supported the right to formalized same-sex relationships, while 39 percent of respondents were against any legal solution. In 2022, the percentage of supporters rose to 62 percent, while the number of opponents dropped to 33 percent. Stowarzyszenia Miłość Nie Wyklucza, "Co o równości myślą Polacy i Polki: Wszystko o badaniach społecznych na temat równości małżeńskiej i akceptacji osób LGBT+,"; https://mnw.org.pl/tematy/badania/ (accessed May 10, 2023).

10 See: George Gasyna, "A Kind of Testament: Reading Witold Gombrowicz as a Transnational Writer," in *A Companion to World Literature*, ed. Ken Seigneurie, 1–10 (Hoboken: Wiley, 2020), 3.

11 Czesław Miłosz, *Rok myśliwego* (Kraków: Społeczny Instytut Wydawniczy Znak, 2001), 278–280.

12 As Gombrowicz puts it, "I am unable to read them. Why? Because they bore me. […] Who knows? This may be why these books are so resistant to criticism. They are so boring so that they are unreadable, so one can't criticize them" (TES 153).

13 George Gasyna, "Rituals at the Limits of Literature: A New Reading of Witold Gombrowicz's *Cosmos*," *The Sarmatian Review*, no. 3 (2007): 1324.

14 Michał P. Markowski, *Czarny nurt: Gombrowicz, świat, literatura* (Kraków: Wydawnictwo Literackie, 2004), 116. Cf. Daniel Pratt, "Narrative and Form: Gombrowicz and the Narrative Conception of Personal Identity," *The Polish Review* 60, no. 2 (2015): 16–20. Gombrowicz himself acknowledges the diminished importance of action and classical linear plot in his works (TES 106).

15 In Gombrowicz works, "[o]ne can emit [utterances] without feeling the threat that someone will respond. The mere awareness that someone is listening is sufficient. […] This is phaticity in its pure form." Janusz Margański, "Gombrowicz i muzyczność," Teksty Drugie, no. 3 (2005): 64. (My translation – AK))

16 Witold Gombrowicz, *Kronos*, ed. Rita Gombrowicz, Jerzy Jarzębski, and Klementyna Suchanow (Kraków: Wydawnictwo Literackie, 2013).

17 Ewa M. Thompson, *Witold Gombrowicz* (Boston: Twayne Publishers, 1979), 121.

18 Quite paradoxically, this highly down-to-earth attitude toward "isms" did not stop Gombrowicz from seeking (and indicating to his readers) some affinities between his literary works and the currently relevant cultural and philosophical streams,

such as existentialism and structuralism (in 1967, he published the paper "I Was a Structuralist Before Anybody Else"). Witold Gombrowicz, "Byłem pierwszym strukturalistą [*J'étais Structuraliste Avant Tout Le Monde*]," in *Gombrowicz filozof*, ed. Francesco M. Cataluccio and Jerzy Illg, 145–154 (Kraków: Społeczny Instytut Wydawniczy Znak, 1991).

19 Michał P. Markowski, "Ze szkoły Montaigne'a," in *Kurs filozofii w sześć godzin i kwadrans*, 5–12 (Kraków: Wydawnictwo Literackie, 2017), 7. (My translation).

20 Ibid., 11.

2 Violence

The Polish-Argentinian novelist, dramaturg, and essayist Witold Marian Gombrowicz was born in 1904 in Małoszyce (then part of the Russian Empire) as the youngest child to a family of the Polish landed gentry (coat of arms: Kościesza) whose roots reached back to the Middle Ages and the Grand Duchy of Lithuania.[1] The habitus of Polish squires, including their vocabulary, family relations, conventional attitudes toward members of other social classes, (empty) rituals, and (curious) traditions, would be visible throughout his entire future literary work, exemplifying the arbitrary artificiality of any social norm, and, at the same time, the frustrating inescapability from the world of forms and interhuman interactions ("from a human being one can only take shelter in the arms of another human being," FER 281).

Witold's father, Jan Onufry Gombrowicz (1868–1933), was a bright figure: despite his noble origins and conservative mentality, in his youth, he was an active supporter of the Polish Socialist Party (*Polska Partia Socjalistyczna*, PPS), whereas later he became a successful entrepreneur who imported and effectively implemented advanced technologies in the newly established family businesses. Witold's mother, Antonina Marcelina née Kotkowska (1872–1959), despite having been raised the fashion typical for women of the gentry, was a sensitive, open-minded personality who managed to combine her deep Catholic faith and conservative upbringing with genuine support for women's liberation.[2] Witold had two older brothers, Janusz and Jerzy, and one older sister, Irena. The Gombrowicz family lived comfortably in the rural region of Lesser Poland (*Małopolska*); in 1911, the entire family moved to Warsaw.

Whereas Witold's early childhood passed in a relatively peaceful time, his early youth was overshadowed by great military conflicts. As a consequence of the First World War (1914–1918), Poland finally gained independence after 123 years of virtual nonexistence on the map of Europe. This did not mean, however, the end of military mobilization, as the final borders of the young state were being formed for half a decade (till 1923) in armed conflicts with almost all its neighboring nations and countries, including Czechoslovakia, Soviet Russia, and Germany. The freshly re-born Poland had to face plenty of internal challenges, beginning with the poverty of its inhabitants. Its industry

DOI: 10.4324/9781003183976-2

Figure 2.1 *Nowy Świat Street in Warsaw on a Summer Day* (1892). Author: Władysław Podkowiński. Public Domain.

was underdeveloped and 70% of the population were peasants, and hence there was an existential need for land reforms. Furthermore, the young state was ethnically, nationally, and confessionally anything but homogenous: "ethnic Poles" constituted less than 70% of society, the rest being Ukrainians (ca. 14%) and Jews (9%), as well as Belarussians, Germans, Tatars, and others; in some rural regions, the local population identified simply as "the natives" (*tutejsi*). Minorities also happened to be internally differentiated and divided, the complex paths of Polish Jews being a good example: they included various factions and sub-factions of Zionists, socialists, communist internationalists, and Orthodox Jews (e.g. *Chassidim*), in addition to assimilated Jews who considered themselves Polish. Even the issue of "Polishness" was troublesome, as "being a Pole" held different meanings for each social class (peasants, factory workers, the petite bourgeoisie, the intelligentsia, and the landed gentry). Moreover, those who identified as Poles used to be citizens of the three different empires from which Poland re-emerged in 1918 (Russia, Austria, and Germany); each had a different policy toward the question of nationality, which influenced the way their former citizens conceived of their "Polishness." When years later, in his *Diary*, Gombrowicz smashed the naïve veneration of national identity, he noticed that "a Pole does not know how to act toward Poland, it confuses him and makes him mannered. [...] Poland forces him into a cramped state—he wants to help it too much, he wants to elevate it too much" (D 7).

In 1918, the 14-year-old Gombrowicz welcomed the dissolution of the prewar orders and hierarchies with a juvenile fascination. Yet the social uncertainty caused by the disappearance of the "old world" and the general exhaustion of the people (after the First World War, Eastern and Central Europe experienced not only the Spanish flu but also the typhus pandemic), together with the consequences of the volatile global economic situation (such as the Great Depression of 1929), resulted in social hostilities, obscurantism, anti-Semitism, and growing political radicalizations. Less than one week after assuming office, the first president of the newly established Republic of Poland was assassinated by a nationalist fanatic; in 1926, the legally elected president and prime minister were forced to resign due to a military *coup d'état*. (At the time, Gombrowicz's family lived only a few streets away from the avenue where the fighting took place.) On the other hand, despite all these difficulties and traumata, Polish intellectual life blossomed in the interwar period. Warsaw and Lviv (then a Polish city) were important centers of mathematics, logic, and philosophy. Researchers who after the Second World War became leading figures at American, Israeli, and European universities, such as Stanisław Ulam (1909–1984), Alfred Tarski (1901–1983), Ludwik Fleck (1896–1961), Jan Łukasiewicz (1989–1956), and the future Nobel Peace Prize winner Joseph (Józef) Rotblat (1908–2005), contributed to the Polish humanities and science. In the early thirties, a group of Polish mathematicians and cryptographers laid the foundations for deciphering the Enigma code the German military used during the Second World War. By the same token, the intense years 1918–1939 were remarkably fruitful for Polish culture; it suffices to mention the flourishing avant-garde art and art theory (Stanisław I. Witkiewicz [1885–1939], Leon Chwistek [1884–1944], Władysław Strzemiński [1893–1952], Katarzyna Kobro [1898–1952]), and literature (Bruno Schulz [1892–1939], Zofia Nałkowska [1884–1954], and the poets of the *Skamander* group). Poland was also the European center of Yiddish culture, including Yiddish theater, cabaret, and cinematography.

A particular exemplification of the intensity and heterogeneity of interwar cultural life in Poland was its capital, Warsaw. Apart from various literary groups and circles (the escapist *Skamander*, the socially engaged *Kadra*, the avant-garde *Klub Artystyczny "S,"* and the Jewish futuristic *Halastre*), the most profound Polish literary weekly, *Wiadomości Literackie* (Literary News) was published in Warsaw. Founded in 1924 and led till 1939 by the assimilated Polish Jew Mieczysław Grydzewski (1894–1970), *Wiadomości* was not only a place where the most talented and popular poets, literary critics, and novelists published their articles on literature and culture, but also an eclectic platform that hosted debates on vital social and political questions (such as the abortion law or the question of capital punishment) and was open to discussing new lifestyle phenomena such as cinema, sports, and tourism. Grydzewski's weekly quickly became known for its leftist-liberal point of view and its attractive and accessible way of presenting serious issues; it thus had an enormous influence on the Polish intelligentsia and the slowly emerging Polish urban bourgeoisie with a centrist-progressive worldview.[3] Gombrowicz would later make some allusions to several concepts discussed in *Wiadomości* in his *Diary* and prose (particularly in the novel *Ferdydurke*).

At the same time, *Wiadomości* was regarded, not without good reason, as an over-rated clique, as Grydzewski was also the editor-in-chief of *Skamander*, the monthly of the *Skamander* literary group, which clearly influenced which authors and topics were endorsed in *Wiadomości*. Throughout the 1920s and 1930s, the authors associated with those two titles became an intrinsic part of the Warsaw circles of influential intelligentsia and high society; some of them unquestionably belonged to the Polish political and financial elites. Finally, the entertaining way of presenting serious issues in *Wiadomości* was considered superficial. Particularly for the generation of authors debuting in the thirties (such as the future Nobel Prize winner Czesław Miłosz), Grydzewski's milieu represented the irritating escapist liberal ignorance that was both unable and unwilling to consider vital contemporary dilemmas in a deeper way.[4]

Gombrowicz's relationship with *Wiadomości* and *Skamander* was, in that respect, more complex. Some progressive ideas promoted in the weekly (such as pacifism) were mercilessly ridiculed in his debut novel *Ferdydurke*; on the other hand—the very first fragments of this work (as well as some other literary pieces) were published precisely in *Skamander*, whereas the book itself received an enthusiastic review in *Wiadomości*.[5] As an aspiring writer, Gombrowicz surreptitiously admired the clear and vibrant style of the leading authors of *Wiadomości*, especially Tadeusz Boy-Żeleński (1874–1941), and Antoni Słonimski (1895–1976),[6] and considered being published in *Skamander* synonymous with unquestionable success in the literary world. At the same time, he remained highly skeptical of the very concept of a literary milieu and the mechanisms of gaining its favor.

In 1933, Gombrowicz published in Warsaw his prose debut, a collection of experimental short stories entitled ***Recollections from Adolescence*** (expanded in 1957 and renamed ***Bacacay***). The volume's reception was not negative, however, as the initial title suggested the focus on the question of immaturity (*Pamiętnik z okresu dojrzewania*, literally: "A Memoir from the Period of Maturing"), the book was not taken as seriously as the young and ambitious author would have liked. Gombrowicz's bizarre and grotesque style and the omnipresence of violence and cruelty were seen as a juvenile attempt to *épater la bourgeoisie*. In fact, in his prewar works, Gombrowicz refuses to spare not only his characters, but also his readers, as apart from depicting scenes of brutality and maliciousness he introduces his own language of all-encompassing hostility, in which he mixes the phraseologies of the Polish upper and lower strata with racial and class slurs, anti-Semitic slogans, and the Polish prewar discourse of "exoticism" and "wildernesses" in the context of Africa and Asia.[7] Ewa M. Thompson notes that Gombrowicz's literary world "arises out of grim struggle,"[8] particularly visible in his short stories: "As a result of this emphasis on a system of attitudes rather than people and events, the protagonists of these stories tend to be flat. [...] 'Dominate or be dominated' is the motto of these characters."[9] Gombrowicz himself explained in 1933 the amount of abhorrence in his debut volume by pointing out that brutality was part of the daily experience: "the predominance [...] of cruelty and revulsion comes from the fact that, in my opinion, their role in life exceeds our wildest dreams. I invoke Hitler in this regard."[10]

Parallel to the atmosphere of absurd violence, in his early works Gombrowicz introduces a plethora of details that show him to be an insightful and disillusioned observer of the ruthlessness of human relationships in the poor, post-feudal Polish society of the interwar period. Even if social questions rather constitute a background to the personal troubles of the main characters, they are nonetheless pervasive. In the story "Dinner at Countess Pavahoke's," a peasant boy dies of cold and starvation watching through a window of the Pavahokes residence a group of squires enjoying an extraordinarily light and elegant dinner (the boy's family name is Cauliflower; cauliflower is also the main dish served during the evening). Gombrowicz (who himself was a great snob) meticulously portrays in "Dinner" the indolence and intellectual idleness of the aristocracy, leaving no doubt that in his eyes this class of people existed solely thanks to the power of social habits and traditional forms of behavior.

The story "On the Kitchen Steps," by contrast, focuses on relations between an energetic middle-class couple and their lower-class handmaids and servants.[11] (In a time of cheap labor and the nonexistence of dishwashers, vacuum cleaners, and washing machines, hiring a maid was a bourgeois standard, not a luxury.) On the one hand, Gombrowicz derides the vulgarity, lack of hygiene, and primitivism of "maids of all work" (*służące do wszystkiego*), while on the other, he also depicts how mercilessly they are exploited and how easily they can fall victim to sexual harassment in the workplace. To quote a phrase of Alexander Etkind's, Gombrowicz portrays lower-class people "as creatures of a fundamentally different nature" to that of their employers,[12] which in "On the Kitchen Steps" is emphasized by the handmaid Czesia's lament: "The mistress doesn't think a maid is a human being!" (BAC 235).

In some of his other stories, Gombrowicz introduces the aesthetics of a surreal nightmare, particularly in the texts in which the protagonists are victims of someone else's brutality. The main hero of "Five Minutes Before Falling Asleep" (renamed "Adventures" in the 1957 edition) is persecuted by a strange "white black man" (*biały Murzyn*) who owns a yacht and wants to kill him, whereas the main character of "The Events on the 'Banbury'" becomes an object of malicious games between the captain and the lieutenant:

> "If those are your orders, captain," said Smith, and he took my hand warmly and squeezed it as if [it were] in a pair of pincers (I once had my hand shaken in just this way by a certain sergeant on land—first warmly, then very strongly)—"in that case we'll knock together a big fishing pole, we'll stick Mr. Zantman on a hook and with this bait we'll catch a great deep water fish. The fish will swallow Mr. Zantman, and we'll slit open its belly and pull him out still alive, like Jonah. It'll be a capital lark. You remember, captain, we got up to worse tricks in the Caribbean Bay—now that was the real thing—ho, ho…"
>
> (BAC 150)

The absurd cruelty is also initiated by Gombrowicz's protagonists: in the story "A Premeditated Crime," the main character, without any reason, psychologically torments the son of a man who died naturally from a heart attack; as a result, the son experiences a mental breakdown and claims to have committed patricide.[13] Finally, in the short story "The Memoirs of Stefan Czarniecki,"[14] Gombrowicz exposes the absurd mechanisms of school education, particularly the "patriotic" upbringing (venerating violence as heroism, the brainless reciting of "patriotic" poetry),[15] as well as the brutal rules of the socialization of the youth (in Gombrowicz's fictional world, children and teenagers are never innocent; they happen to be crueler than adults). The hero, Czarniecki, desperately and unsuccessfully seeks acceptance at school, from his colleagues, and, later, from girls, whereas his parents are mostly busy hating each other (his father is a dandy Polish nobleman and an anti-Semite, his mother an ugly Jewish woman who converted to Christianity and became a Polish Catholic bigot). Being half-Polish, half-Jewish, Czarniecki experiences, in every milieu, different kinds of racist micro-aggressions (half-smiles, indiscrete yet intent staring at his nose) which together with the later trauma of serving in the military effectively damage his psyche. Ultimately, Czarniecki identifies as "a communist" (although his understanding of "communism" is somewhat bizarre: "I demand [...] that my mother be cut into pieces and that anyone who is not a fervent prayer be given a piece," BAC 32) and declares a grotesque war on society: "[W]henever it is virtue or family, faith or fatherland, I always have to commit some villainy" (BAC 34).[16]

Literary critics noticed Gombrowicz's book debut, but the reviews, while positive, were lukewarm in tone and rather superficial.[17] Unfortunately for Gombrowicz, his absurd and sarcastic re-usage of the blatant anti-Semitic stereotypes and slogans (such as "*Dieu pardonnera, les hommes oublieront, mais le nez restera,*" BAC 21) was read at the time of politicized violence and hostility not as an attempt to question hierarchies and myths of homogenous identities, but in a flat and literal way. Decades after the war, Gombrowicz complained that "The Memoirs of Stefan Czarniecki" was enthusiastically welcomed by a flamboyant Warsaw anti-Semite, Adolf Nowaczyński (1876–1944), whose praise should have automatically caused a cold distance among more progressive and socially engaged circles who were not interested in exploring the nuances of the debut experimental prose of an unknown author (PM 125–126). That was not entirely accurate, since Gombrowicz's prewar short stories, essays, articles, and reportages were published by various Polish journals and newspapers, including the leftist liberal *Wiadomości*. Still, the suspicion of anti-Semitism must have hurt, as Gombrowicz's attitude toward Jews was sincerely free of resentment; his modest circle of friends included the Polish-Jewish poet Zuzanna Ginczanka (1917–1944) and the magnificent Polish-Jewish writer and artist Bruno Schulz (1892–1942). As he pointed out in his memories, he was simply raised this way, for in his family anti-Semitism was perceived as "a sign of narrow-mindedness" (PM 177). And even though Gombrowicz did indeed share some popular convictions and myths of his own social class (for instance the notion that "the anti-Semitism of the [Polish] gentry was not dangerous"),[18] unlike many of his Polish compatriots at the time he was able to notice and acknowledge the painful and bitter battle Eastern European Jews had to fight in a rapidly modernizing, disenchanted, and hostile world. The realm of traditional and religious Jewry in Poland was shrinking, torn by new ideologies and internal conflicts and attacked from almost all sides of the Polish political spectrum (in *Wiadomości*, it was Antoni Słonimski who never missed an opportunity to mock Orthodox Jews).[19] In addition, Gombrowicz saw the paradox of assimilation described years later by Hannah Arendt: in a predominantly anti-Semitic society, "successful assimilation" is a contradiction in terms, as it requires Jews to adopt an anti-Semitic mindset.[20] As Jews constituted a third of Warsaw's prewar population, Gombrowicz had many opportunities to observe how they struggled to re-define their identities and their place in society and to (literally and metaphorically) "leave the ghetto." In the *Polish Memories*, he explained how this—together with his own experience of originating from a funny and out-of-date class of the Polish nobility[21]—influenced his way of conceiving of issues that later became the leitmotivs of his literary works, particularly the questions of intersubjectivity and "the Form"[22]:

> The ghetto Jews with their beards and gaberdines, the ecstatic poets from the artists' cafés, the millionaires of the stock exchange. Almost all of them were in one way or another grotesque, almost implausible as a phenomenon. And as Jews are intelligent, they sense it but are unable to free themselves from this bad form. And it's because of this that they often feel themselves to be a caricature, an eccentric joke of the Creator. This tension in the Jew's relation to form; the fact that it torments him so, or renders him laughable, or humiliates him; the fact that a Jew is never fully himself in a way that a peasant or a squire is himself, thoroughly comfortable in a form he has inherited from preceding generations; the fact that a Jew always has to be some compromise of form and its catastrophe; all this made the Jews fascinating to me.
>
> (PM 178–179)

The suffering of an individual who must fight for his identity in an unraveling and uncanny world is one of the major themes of Gombrowicz's debut novel, *Ferdydurke*.

Figure 2.2 Street Corner in the Jewish Quarter in Warsaw (1934). Author: Willem van de Poll. CC 0.

Ferdydurke was Gombrowicz's first novel, yet it is considered to be his most important piece of prose and one of the most seminal works of twentieth-century Polish literature, enthusiastic recipients including Milan Kundera (1929–2023) and Susan Sontag (1933–2004). Its first fragment was published in 1935 in *Skamander*[23]; as a novel it was issued in 1937 (in 1938, according to its publisher), immediately becoming a literary sensation.[24] *Ferdydurke* was praised as an "outstanding intellectual act: cognitive and ethical."[25] The novel was greeted excitedly by Bruno Schulz, who pointed out its Freudian motives as well as its insightful analyses of contemporary culture.[26] The enigmatic title is not intended to mean anything (the English title of the film adaptation of 1991 is *30 Door Key*).[27] As Bogdan Baran and Henryk Markiewicz showed, Gombrowicz borrowed the name "Freddy Durkee" from the satirical novel *Babbit* (1922) by Sinclair Lewis (1885–1951), the Nobel laureate of 1930.[28]

Summarizing the absurd plot of *Ferdydurke* is no easy task. The novel's central character and first-person narrator, the 30-year-old Joey, becomes a plaything of various Form-givers, such as professors, elderly family members, and bossy teenagers. After a visit by a dominant pedagogue, Professor Pimko, who treats him like a teenager for no apparent reason, Joey suddenly finds himself *becoming* a teenager and, despite his protests, is forced to return to school. Unlike Franz Kafka's *Metamorphosis* (1915), Joey's unexpected transformation is not physical; it is sufficient that those around him follow Pimko's way of considering Joey as a teenage boy who is "posturing a bit, pretending to be an adult" (FER 111). On the other hand, the time passes, Joey involuntarily begins to exhibit typical behavior patterns of sulky teenagers. *Ferdydurke* is thus a grotesque anti-*Bildungsroman* (antinovel of education), as the development of the main hero goes in the opposite direction and the very idea of maturity is questioned: people do not mature by themselves; it is a social ideal of maturity that is imposed on them,[29] often against their will and by forceful means.

The form of *Ferdydurke* is characterized by a heterogeneous structure and style, which increases the overall effect of absurdity and disorientation. The work incorporates elements of fiction and nonfiction, including literary criticism (in part a commentary on the novel itself), and the philosophical essay format.[30] Additionally, two short stories, published earlier in the volume *Recollections from Adolescence*, are also included in the novel, despite having no direct bearing on the main plot.[31] The *Ferdydurke*'s style is further characterized by clashes of diverse linguistic registers, including the language of the lower classes, peasants, and students, and slogans of progressive newspapers. Moreover, the novel contains instances of common words and phrases that are given new and unexpected meanings, exemplified by the word "mug" (*gęba*), which takes on the sense of someone's established social role, often unwanted or the result of a misunderstanding or a coincidence. Another striking feature of the novel's style is mixing the grotesque with elements of realism,[32] as well as using allusions to various social phenomena of the interwar period, such as the rise of fascism and other radical movements.[33] Finally, Gombrowicz parodies in his work various figures of Polish cultural life, for instance the Marxist literary critic Ignacy Fik (1904–1942).[34]

Twenty years after publishing *Ferdydurke*, Gombrowicz summarized its main ideas and theoretical concepts:

> [M]y man is created from the outside, that is, he is inauthentic in essence—he is always not-himself, because he is determined by form, which is born between people. His "I," therefore, is marked for him in that "interhumanity." An eternal actor, but a natural one, because his artificiality is inborn, it makes up a feature of his humanity—to be a man means to be an actor—to be a man means to pretend to be a man—to be a man means to "act like" a man while not being one deep inside—to be a man is to recite humanity. [...] If I can never be entirely myself, the only thing that allows me to save my personality from annihilation is my will to authenticity, that stubborn-in-spite-of-everything "I want to be myself," which is nothing more than a tragic and hopeless revolt against deformation. I cannot be myself, yet I want to be myself and I must be myself—this is the antinomy, one of those that do not let themselves be resolved... and do not expect me to provide you with medicine for incurable diseases.
>
> (D 288–289)

This is how *Ferdydurke* was (and still is) understood, not only by avid readers but also by the majority of critics. The forceful reduction of Joey to a teenager and his battles with "the Form" are seen as calling into question every social and cultural norm on the one hand and examining the notion of authenticity on the other. As Bruno Schulz put it, "Gombrowicz opposes the fundamental trend of culture, which is based on man's perpetual subsistence on a diet of some portions, ideologies, banalities, or forms extrapolated from himself, rather than on his own living for himself, through his own integral totality, through the gist of himself."[35]

However, Joey's struggle against the external powers that constantly try to dominate him and reshape his personality is not innocent. Joey has no objections to manipulating or even hurting other people and animals, as in his eyes his absurd enslavement allows him to resort to any means. For instance, he has no qualms about rummaging through Zuta's personal belongings in her room or arranging situations that will put her in distress.[36] This is one of the further paradoxes of *Ferdydurke*: Joey feels trapped in a role of a youngster, but his impulsive and thoughtless behavior reflects the behavior of a teenager whose painful experience of adolescence process partially diminishes their capacity for empathy and consideration toward others. In this perspective, violence and cruelty, along with the authentic joy felt by the perpetrator, are ineliminable, as they constitute physiologically determined

Figure 2.3 *Dedication* [self-portrait] (1920/1922). Author: Bruno Schulz. Public Domain. Bruno Schulz (1892–1942) was a Polish-Jewish writer and artist who admired and keenly endorsed Gombrowicz's early literary work.

elements of human life. This illustrates well the ruthless relationships between students at school: Joey does not protest when his schoolmates rape their peer; moreover, he summarizes the later suicide of the raped boy with a cynical rhetorical question ("Syphon died, so what?," FER 133) and a cheap wordplay.[37]

Joey's teen-like cynicism is particularly visible in the last part of the novel, when the plot moves to the rural residence (*dwór*) of the Polish landed gentry, where he and his schoolmate Kneadus are hosted as distant relatives. Whereas in his earlier short story "Dinner at Countess Pavahoke's," the realm of the Polish nobility is presented from an outsider's perspective (the narrator is a bourgeois, for whom an invitation from a countess is an unusual honor), in *Ferdydurke* Joey is an insider: he knows perfectly the codes of behavior, particularly those that concern the relationships between the lord of the manor and his family and the peasants and manor workers. Joey is painfully aware not only of the glaring inequality and injustice of those relationships, but also of the fact that in the twentieth century, they are embarrassingly out of date. Nonetheless, he demonstrates his subjectivity not by questioning, but rather by following the traditional way of maltreating servants, which includes acts of regular violence, such as beating and punching them in the face without any reason, just to underscore the existing hierarchy.

> "[A] guy like Valek will respect you like his lord and master if you hit him in the snoot. You have to know the likes of them! They love it! […] In times past, my father and uncle Severyn used to hit the doorman at the Grand Hotel in the snoot." "And our uncle Eustachy," I said, "once hit his barber in the snoot." "No one hit the snoot as well as grandma Evelina, but that belongs to the past. Well, Toby Patz got drunk and smacked a train conductor in the snoot. Do you know Pavel Patz, he's very unaffected."
>
> (FER 225)

In this part of the novel, Gombrowicz introduces a caricatured yet, in its essence, realistic portrait of the situation of the peasants and lower classes in rural Poland before the Second World War.[38]

In Gombrowicz's later works, cruelty and violence slowly gain more moral weight, ceasing to be treated in a flat and blasé manner as in *Ferdydurke* and the early short stories. The contemporary writer Stefan Chwin (1949–) proposes a comparison between how the motif of suicide is conceptualized

Figure 2.4 The Gombrowicz Mansion in Wsola, Poland (2018). Author: Aleksandra Konarzewska. In Wsola, Gombrowicz worked on the novel *Ferdydurke*.

in *Ferdydurke* and in Gombrowicz's drama play *The Marriage* (1948). In the former work, killing oneself is an occasion for making cruel, teen-style jokes, while in the latter, it is a tragedy that makes the marriage ceremony impossible.[39] In Gombrowicz's postwar oeuvre, the focus moves slowly toward acknowledging actual physical pain in both human and nonhuman beings. The grotesque novella *Trans-Atlantyk* (1953) still features the motif of kidnapping, planning a murder, and using physical violence, but in the novel *Pornografia* (1960), the killing of an innocent worm by two teenagers announces four upcoming homicides. Finally, in Gombrowicz's last novel, *Cosmos*, killing animals (a bird and a cat) becomes a metaphysical felony.

In his *Diary*, the 54-year-old Gombrowicz confesses, "In my youth I tortured animals. [...] Today I am afraid—this is the right word—of the suffering of a fly" (D 311). In the same work, there are also questions about the general human acceptance of exploiting, tormenting, and killing animals.[40] In Gombrowicz's eyes, one of the main weaknesses of leading postwar streams in literature and philosophy (such as the French *Nouveau Roman*, Marxism, existentialism, and Roman Catholic theology)[41] lies in their stubborn anthropocentrism that refuses to consider a human being as only one of the many elements of the real world and is unwilling to acknowledge the issue of physical pain as a genuine philosophical question.

Notes

1 In the nineteenth century, due to the Russian persecutions after the failed January Uprising, Gombrowicz's grandfather was forced to leave his native Lithuania and settle with his family in Lesser Poland (*Małopolska*).

2 In his memories, Gombrowicz portrays his mother primarily as a neurotic and mentally unbalanced upper-class lady. Klementyna Suchanow shows how unjust this description is: Klementyna Suchanow, *Gombrowicz: Ja, geniusz*, 2 vols. (Wołowiec: Wydawnictwo Czarne, 2017), I 66–75.

3 Małgorzata Szpakowska, *"Wiadomości Literackie" prawie dla wszystkich* (Warszawa: Wydawnictwo W.A.B, 2012).

4 Cf. Miłosz's opinion and literary journalism of that time: Czesław Miłosz, *Przygody młodego umysłu: Publicystyka i proza 1931–1939*, ed. Agnieszka Stawiarska (Kraków: Społeczny Instytut Wydawniczy Znak, 2003).

5 Szpakowska, *"Wiadomości Literackie" prawie dla wszystkich*, 262.

6 See D 202–203.

7 As Poland never possessed overseas colonies, the Polish prewar discourse of "exoticism" was copied 1:1 from the English and French colonial discourses, which in Polish settings often had an unintentionally funny effect that was easy to mock. Gombrowicz makes use of this, turning up the spiral of absurdity to extremes: "It is not without a deeper meaning that those far-off lands are called virgin lands where the men wear plaits, where ears weighed down by metal earrings stretch to the shoulders, and where beneath the baobab tree idols devour slaves or infants, while the entire population indulges in ritual contortions. Is a kiss by rubbing noses, as practiced among the savage tribes, not something taken directly from an innocent dreamy little head?" (BAC 109–110).

8 Thompson, *Witold Gombrowicz*, 22.

9 Ibid., 36.

10 My translation. Originally in Polish: *[P]rzewaga [...] okrucieństwa i wstrętu wynika stąd, że, moim zdaniem, rola ich w życiu przewyższa nasze najśmielsze marzenia. Powołuję się w tym względzie na Hitlera.* Witold Gombrowicz, "Krótkie objaśnienie," in *Bakakaj*, ed. Jan Błoński, 194–196, Dzieła 1 (Kraków: Wydawnictwo Literackie, 1986), 196.

11 This short story was first published in 1937 in *Skamander* and included in the volume *Bacacay* in 1957.

12 Alexander Etkind, *Internal Colonization: Russia's Imperial Experience* (Cambridge, Malden: Polity Press, 2011), 232. Etkind writes on Russian literature, but the tendency described by him was present in the Polish culture as well.

13 Silvia G. Dapía, "The Anatomy of Feeling in Gombrowicz's *A Premeditated Crime* (*Zbrodnia z premedytacją*)," in *Gombrowicz in Transnational Context: Translation, Affect, and Politics*, ed. Silvia G. Dapía, 169–184 (New York: Routledge, 2019).

14 Initially: "The Short Memoirs of Jakub Czarniecki." In the 1957 edition, the title was changed.

15 Tomasz Jativa, "Form and Power: On the Disciplinary Coding of National Identity in "Pamiętnik Stefana Czarnieckiego" by Witold Gombrowicz," *Czytanie Literatury. Łódzkie Studia Literaturoznawcze*, no. 9 (2020).

16 Bożena Umińska-Keff writes that *The Memoirs of Stefan Czarniecki* "[s]hows how the external signs of otherness lead to gaining, developing an internal critical alienation, and how this type of alienation, in turn, allows one to undermine existing myths, orders and hierarchies" (trans. Marcin Tereszewski). Bożena Umińska, *Postać z cieniem: Portrety Żydówek w polskiej literaturze od końca XIX wieku do 1939 roku* (Warsaw: Wydawnictwo Sic!, 2001), 276, quoted in: Błażej Warkocki, "A Queer Construction of Identity in the *Memoir of Stefan Czarniecki* by Witold Gombrowicz," *Central Europe* 19, no. 1 (2021): 37.

17 Łukasz Garbal, *Ferdydurke: Biografia powieści* (Kraków: Towarzystwo Autorów i Wydawców Prac Naukowych "Universitas," 2010), 23–26.

18 "And in any case, the anti-Semitism of the gentry was not dangerous: The 'destructive role' of the Jews was criticized, but every squire had his Jew with whom he would sit on the verandah for hours in secret conversations testifying to a coexistence that had lasted for centuries." (PM 177). Cf. Knut A. Grimstad, "What Jews Meant to Witold Gombrowicz, or: Philosemitism as a Strategy for Identity Formation," *The Slavonic and East European Review* 95, no. 4 (2017).

19 Słonimski criticized Orthodox Jewry for its assumed bigotry and obscurantism from an atheist-progressive position. He himself was a Polish Jew and a convinced leftist whose grandfather and great-grandfather were famous scientists and the representatives of the broadly understood *Haskalah* (the Jewish Enlightenment).

20 Hannah Arendt, *Rahel Varnhagen: Lebensgeschichte einer deutschen Jüdin aus der Romantik* (Munich: Piper, 1959); 208.

21 For the argument that a figure of symmetry between 'being a Jew' and 'being a (funny) nobleman' is a troublesome one, see: István Eörsi, "Mój czas z Gombrowiczem," *Literatura na Świecie* 357, no. 4 (2001): 97.

22 See: Jean-Pierre Salgas, *Witold Gombrowicz ou l'athéisme généralisé* (Paris: Édition du Seuil, 2000), 69–70. Cf. Giovana Tomassucci, "'I Owed a Great Deal to Them': Some Hypotheses About the Paradoxes of Jewish Assimilation in Gombrowicz's Works," *pl.it – rassegna italiana di argomenti polacchi*, no. 11 (2020); Suchanow, *Gombrowicz*, I 317.

23 Witold Gombrowicz, "Ferdydurke," in *Czytelnicy i krytycy: Proza, reportaże, krytyka literacka, eseje, przedmowy*, ed. Włodzimierz Bolecki, 47–76, Varia 1 (Kraków: Wydawnictwo Literackie, 2004).

24 Garbal, *Ferdydurke*, 58–68; 149–166.
25 Ludwik Fryde, "O 'Ferdydurke' Gombrowicza," in *Gombrowicz i krytycy*, ed. Zdzisław Łapiński, 57–69 (Kraków, Wrocław: Wydawnictwo Literackie, 1984), 59.
26 Bruno Schulz, "Ferdydurke," *Literary Studies in Poland* 10, no. 1983. Schulz was also the illustrator of the first edition of the book. Cf. Suchanow, *Gombrowicz*, I 300–304, 327–329.
27 Jerzy Skolimowski, *30 Door Key: Ferdydurke* (1991).
28 Henryk Markiewicz, "Do Genezy 'Ferdydurke'," *Teksty Drugie* 6 (2004). See also: Daniel W. Pratt, ""Freddy Durkee" and "Ferdydurke": A Gombrowiczian Reading of "Babbitt"," *Comparative Literature Studies* 52, no. 3 (2015).
29 Konstanty A. Jeleński, "Bohaterskie niebohaterstwo Gombrowicza," in *Chwile oderwane*, ed. Piotr Kłoczowski, 35–50 (Gdańsk: słowo/obraz terytoria, 2010), 46.
30 Michał Głowiński, "Gombrowiczowska diatryba," *Pamiętnik Literacki*, no. 4 (2000): 64.
31 Garbal, *Ferdydurke*, 13, 213.
32 Marcel Reich-Ranicki, "Geknebelt, geschulmeistert, verpaukert: Die Parabel vom Untergang des Intellektuellen. Der schwarze Humor eines Mannes aus Polen," in *Ein Patagonier in Berlin: Texte der deutschen Gombrowicz-Rezeption*, ed. Marek Zybura, 45–48 (Dresden: Neisse Verlag, 2018), 46.
33 Garbal, *Ferdydurke*, 136–144; Andrzej S. Kowalczyk, "'Their Astounding Strength in Overcoming Their Past…': The Memory of Nazism in the Berlin Diary," in *Gombrowicz in Transnational Context: Translation, Affect, and Politics, ed. Silvia G. Dapía*, 208–24 (New York: Routledge, 2019), 208–214; Klara Lutsky, "'I Know What I Am Not': The Problem of the Marginal Self in Gombrowicz's Novels," *The Polish Review* 60, no. 2 (2015): 23–24; Jerzy Jarzębski, "Gombrowicz's Wild Youth: The 'Ferdydurkean Individual' Fades Away," in *Gombrowicz in Transnational Context: Translation, Affect, and Politics*, ed. Silvia G. Dapía, 187–207 (New York: Routledge, 2019).
34 Garbal, *Ferdydurke*, 40–47.
35 Schulz, "Ferdydurke,": 30.
36 Stefan Chwin, "Grzechy Gombrowicza przeciwko wolności: O projekcie etycznym wpisanym w *Ferdydurke*," *Przestrzenie Teorii*, no. 20 (2013): 13–14.
37 In Polish: *powiesił się na wieszaku*. This wordplay is lost in the English translation ("he hanged himself from a coat rack"). As the Polish writer Stefan Chwin writes, this dismissive pun turned the seriousness of suicide into "a slapstick gag from a Chaplin movie." Ibid., 18.
38 Konstanty A. Jeleński, "Dział wód," in *Chwile oderwane*, ed. Piotr Kłoczowski, 92–5 (Gdańsk: słowo/obraz terytoria, 2010); Michał Legierski, *Modernizm Witolda Gombrowicza* (Warszawa: Instytut Badań Literackich PAN, 1999), 70–74.
39 Chwin, "Grzechy Gombrowicza przeciwko wolności,": 22–23.
40 See: Włodzimierz Bolecki, "'Jak zachować się wobec krowy?': (Wstęp do bestiarium Witolda Gombrowicza)," in *Bestiarium*, ed. Włodzimierz Bolecki, 7–18 (Kraków: Wydawnictwo Literackie, 2004); Monika Żołkoś, "Gombrowicz w świecie zwierząt," *Dialog* 651, no. 2 (2011).
41 Czesław Miłosz, "Przyrodnik," *Miesięcznik ZNAK* 579, no. 8 (2003): 19.

3 Eroticism

Ewa Thompson has rightly stated that Gombrowicz's literary universe is a "loveless world."[1] The reader of his works will search in vain for stories of a deep emotional bond between two persons or a protagonist who would be able to love someone so profoundly and innocently as, say, Juliet loved Romeo. A lack of love, however, does not imply a lack of eroticism; on the contrary, the question of human sexuality is one of the most important motifs in Gombrowicz's literary oeuvre.

In the preface to his debut collection of short stories (which was eventually not included in the volume), Gombrowicz explains that "[a]s far as the sexual factor, in particular, is concerned, its predominance is due to the spirit of the times, which unfortunately increasingly accentuates the connection between the sexual sphere and the spiritual sphere […]."[2] In his prewar prose pieces, he presents sexuality calmly and not without sarcasm, as if his main aim were an investigative exploration of certain properties that cause various sexual interests and drives.[3] There are motifs of masochism, an obsession with a stranger, stalking, the sexual fetishization of people from the lower classes, and the motif of attempts at grooming ("Lawyer Kraykowski's Dancer," "The Events on the Banbury," "On the Kitchen Steps," and *Ferdydurke*). In most cases, the erotic appeal is linked to the attributes of social status: the hero in "Lawyer Kraykowski's Dancer" is fascinated by Kraykowski's dandy manners and outfits; in *Ferdydurke*, Zuta Youngblood's teenage sex appeal results largely from her modern, gadget-based lifestyle that in fact defines her personality.[4] Zuta attracts not only her classmate Kopyrda, but also much older men, including the 30-year-old Joey and Professor Pimko (the latter abuses his authority as a teacher in the hope of having an affair with her, FER 162–163).

The ladder of social hierarchy, however, is often turned upside down, as the sexual attractiveness in Gombrowicz's prewar works can also result from a lack of education and civility, from abominable physical attributes (such as bad teeth), or from sheer ugliness. Filip, the protagonist of the short story "On the Kitchen Steps," is not fond of neat and elegant salon ladies, preferring "the most unsightly drudges, misshapen, bloodshot, or overweight,

DOI: 10.4324/9781003183976-3

with horrendous backsides, broken noses" (BAC 218). Being a successful and wealthy man and a member of the Warsaw elite, he is ashamed of his fetish.

> If only it had been baldness. If only it had been baldness – as they say, a young girl, or a night on the town, or a private room at the restaurant and then to a hotel, something merry, something flashy, I'd pay no heed to the tittle-tattle and would simply say that I was a wolf. But since it was bashfulness, what could I do, how could I defend myself, how could I explain myself? [...] I was afraid of ridicule.
>
> (BAC 219)

Whereas Filip tries—at least to some extent—to hide his preferences from people who surround him, Prince Philip in the play *Princess Ivona* (1938) spontaneously decides to marry an unattractive and clumsy Ivona just to rebel against the usual rules of erotic magnetism.

> 'Am I not rich enough to take on this misery? Why, pray, should only prettiness attract me. Who says so? What is wrong with being ugly? Is there a law against it? Even if it were the law, I would not follow it blindly. I am free.'
>
> (PLA 24)

The inverted reverted hierarchy of desire also appears in the novel *Ferdydurke*, where Gombrowicz introduces the figure of a teenager from a middle-class background nicknamed Kneadus (*Miętus*; *miętosić* meaning "to knead"), whose only desire is to find a genuine peasant farmhand (*parobek*) with whom he could "fra.ternize" (*pobra.tać się,* one of many Gombrowiczian plays with spelling). As in the case of "On the Kitchen Steps," the unusual sexual preference reverts the established social hierarchy: because of their burning desires, Filip and Kneadus turn out to be vulnerable and—at least in their own perception—are deprived of their privileged social status, as their happiness depends solely on the presence and acceptance of handmaids and farm workers. Needless to say, such preferences and "unnatural" interests in physically unattractive, lower-class people raise serious concerns and objections from their milieu, in which they are considered ridiculous and irresponsible. When Kneadus' schoolmates catch him dreaming of a farmhand, he immediately becomes the subject of vicious teenage derision:

> 'Congratulations, Kneadalski! Now we know what's going on! We've caught you, my friend, with your pants down! So you're hankering after a farmhand, are you?! You'd like to go trotting with a farmhand over a meadow, would you?! You pretend to be a realist, a brute, you fight the idealism of others, while deep down you're a sentimentalist yourself. A farmhand sentimentalist!'
>
> (FER 53)

Whereas the way of depicting erotic interactions characteristic of Gombrowicz's prewar writings is rather analytical, in his later works, particularly in *Trans-Atlantyk*, *Pornografia*, and vast parts of the *Diary*, the question of eroticism becomes conceptualized in a different way: the lovelessness is still present, but sexual drives cease to be reduced to being objects of a cold investigation only; there appear moments when eroticism is combined with sincere delight and joy. Interestingly, all those works were written during his exile in Argentina, where he lived for almost a quarter of the century.

Gombrowicz found himself in Buenos Aires in the late August of 1939 by sheer coincidence.[5] In 1938, he traveled through Austria, where he witnessed the triumph of Nazism. Since then, he was deeply aware of the inevitability of the next great military conflict in Europe, as well as the unfortunate, very central location of Poland in such an event ("The worst of it is there's no place to run!," POR 12). Poland bordered the Soviet Union to the East and Nazi Germany to the West; in the late thirties, neither country hid its appetite for conquest. Hence when Gombrowicz was made an offer to travel to South America and write a reportage about a new Polish ocean liner, he did not hesitate to accept it. In the summer of 1939, the MS Chrobry left the harbor in Gdynia and reached Buenos Aires in the late August, just as Germany and the Soviet Union sealed their alliance by signing a pact of non-aggression that divided Europe into Hitler's and Stalin's sphere of influences.[6] Gombrowicz's fears proved justified: on September 1, 1939, Germany attacked Poland from

Figure 3.1 Polish Passenger Ship MS Chrobry (1939). Author unknown. Public Domain. MS Chrobry was an ocean liner that operated during the World War II period. It was sunk by German fighter planes in 1940.

the West and less than three weeks later Soviet armed troops annexed a third of the country in the East. After 21 years, the Polish state ceased to exist, conquered by the two totalitarian superpowers.

From that perspective, Gombrowicz was lucky. In the first half of the twentieth century, Argentina was a popular destination for economic migration from Central and Eastern Europe, similar to Brazil and Costa Rica. In 1939, its capital Buenos Aires, was a modern, rapidly developing metropolis of two million with underground lines, skyscrapers, numerous elegant boutiques, private cars, and intense nightlife that hypnotized incoming Europeans ("…there Luxurious shops, an extraordinary abundance of Goods, merchandise, and the flower of distingué society, Houses of fashion, exceeding big, *confiseries*," T-A 4).[7] In the mild yet intense atmosphere of Buenos Aires, Gombrowicz could crystallize his views on literature, philosophy, and sexuality and become a mature, self-aware author. In Argentina, he wrote his drama *The Marriage*, most of his monumental *Diary*, the novels *Trans-Atlantyk*, *Pornography*, and *Cosmos* (although the latter was completed in Europe), as well as his seminal essays (*Sienkiewicz*, *Against Poets*). Ultimately, it was in Argentina that Gombrowicz established deep intellectual and intimate personal relationships (with Juan Carlos Gómez, Alejandro Rússovich, Mariano Betelú), eventually becoming an intrinsic element of Argentinian literary and artistic life in the postwar decades, sometimes compared with Jorge Luis Borges.[8] It should be no surprise

Figure 3.2 Gas station in Chacarita district of Buenos Aires (1951). Author unknown. Public Domain.

that Gombrowicz ultimately referred to Argentina as *la Patria*, his second homeland, a place where he became a professional and successful writer and where he experienced "an eruption of some sort of belated youth" (D 160).

The beginnings, however, were not easy. When Gombrowicz arrived in Argentina, he did not know the language and had neither money nor close friends. As a writer, he was nonexistent, as at that time none of his works had been translated from Polish. Moreover, the leading position in the intellectual life of Buenos Aires was held by the publishing house and journal *Sur*, founded and led by Victoria Ocampo (1890–1979), the writer, translator, cultural manager, feminist, and arts sponsor. *Sur's* publications included works by Jorge Luis Borges, Walter Gropius, José Ortega y Gasset, Octavio Paz, Virginia Woolf, Vladimir Nabokov, Jean-Paul Sartre, and Albert Camus. To some extent, Argentinian authors and sympathizers gathered around *Sur* represented for Gombrowicz everything against which he had always rebelled—intellectual snobbery, the power of literary cliques, and irritating humility toward everything presented as "European" (particularly: "French" or *parisien*). As Juan J. Saer points out, Gombrowicz's philippics against Polish literature and intellectual life in *Diary* refer to Argentinian affairs as well.[9] The Argentinian writers' circles of mutual adoration were humorously portrayed in the *Trans-Atlantyk* (1953), when the novel's protagonist attends a cocktail party:

> Very richly dressed and neat, as shirts of Silk or of Cambric for 13, 14 or even 15 Pesos, ties, Cravats, or modish Lorgnettes, likewise Pumps, then narrow-rimmed Heels, kerchiefs, lip rouges, ankle boots of English style for 20 or 30 Pesos. But primarily Men's socks struck the eye, and by pulling up their trouser legs, they these Socks eagerly shew, whilst ladies do each others' Hats assess. So one pats the other. One the other tenderly embraces: "Amigo, amigo"—"Que tal?"— "Que es de tu vida, que me cuentas?" But despite that tenderness, cordiality, now and then the Discourse subsides or falls off for one speaks and the other in distraction, in some Forgetfulness now has stopped listening, now is inspecting his Sock. So they are saying: "Is that Revista out yet?"— "I was paid 50 Pesos for an article"— "How are you, how are you! What news?"— "How much was that Land?"— "I acquired Socks for myself." Then all together hands raised up and their heads clasping cried aloud: "Oh, what do we Say? Oh, why can we not say our Say?! Oh, why do we not Respect and Honour each other?! Oh, why so Shallow, so Shallow?!" So one to the other Flits, one bestows Honour on the other, one to the other "Maestro, maestro" and "Gran Escritor" and "Que Obra" and "Que Gloria" but what, since it falls off anon and again in distraction they are inspecting Socks.
>
> (T-A 30–31)

On the other hand, Gombrowicz managed to establish some friendly relationships with various Latin American authors (for instance Virgilio Piñera,

Adolfo de Obieta, and Humberto Rodríguez Tomeu), thanks to whom the Spanish edition of *Ferdydurke* in 1947 was possible. The novel's translation process became legendary,[10] both for its disarming lack of professionalism (none of the members of the "translation committee" that gathered in Café Rex spoke Polish or possessed a Polish dictionary, while Gombrowicz's command of Spanish was still intermediate) and for the fact that the ultimate result turned out to be quite satisfying.[11] The translators managed even to "slightly ton[e] down the Polish context and subtly ad[d] some Argentine language, [...] [or] an additional element (like the nudity on the beach) to make sure that the licentiousness of the original comes through."[12] And, as Silvia G. Dapía stresses, it was the Argentinian translation of *Ferdydurke* that opened the door to global acknowledgment, for the literary critic François Bondy, who discovered Gombrowicz's writings for the international audience, read the novel in Spanish.[13]

The first longer piece of prose written by Gombrowicz entirely in Argentina was the novella ***Trans-Atlantyk***. Its initial fragments appeared in 1951 in the journal *Kultura* (as a book, *Trans-Atlantyk* was published two years later, in one volume with the play *The Marriage*) and immediately caused the indignation of Polish readers, as the trauma of the Second World War and the later forceful implementation of Soviet rule was still very fresh.[14] The absurd, semi-autobiographical story of "Witold Gombrowicz," an experimental novelist who in the summer of 1939 arrives in Buenos Aires and instead of fulfilling his patriotic duty becomes involved in an erotic intrigue arranged by a local millionaire who is in love with a Polish teenager, broke all possible taboos.[15] Not only did Gombrowicz present Polish émigrés as pompous losers mentally still living in the past, not only did he confront the bare ideal of the "fatherland" with an alternative counter-value, "Filistria" (*Synczyzna,* literally: "a Sonland"), but he also combined those issues with the questions of sexual obsessions and homosexuality (in Poland, homosexuality had been decriminalized in 1932, but it was still regarded as "unnatural").[16] The peculiar language and style (such as a plethora of neologisms and the arbitrary usage of upper-case letters in the middle of a sentence) together with adopting some fashions of Polish Baroque literature additionally intensified the complexity of the novella. Readers of *Trans-Atlantyk* have to decipher Gombrowicz's facetious intertextual play with the classical works of Polish literature (particularly the poem *Pan Tadeusz* by Adam Mickiewicz) and Polish literary topoi (such as the topos of a rural gentry residence, *dwór*, and its rituals). In his novella, Gombrowicz parodies practices of hound hunting and dueling, brilliantly merging the slowly unraveling world of the Polish nobility with elements of the Argentinian culture of *estancieros* and financial elites. By the same token, the figure of "Walking," with which Witold seeks to demonstrate his individuality ("And more and more my walk strengthens, becomes Mightier... and so the Devil, the Devil, I Walk on and Walk forth and Walk, and so am Walking, Walking and Walking and Walking...," T-A 35), hints at both the traditional Polish dance, the polonaise, and the Argentinian tango.[17] The title *Trans-Atlantyk* can be read as "across the Atlantic Ocean" (this meaning was suggested by Gombrowicz himself, as it suggests a literal and metaphorical transgression and translocation, TES 111), although in Polish the word *transantlyk* means no more than an "ocean liner."

The focal moment of *Trans-Atlantyk* is when Witold becomes acquainted with Arturo Gonzalo ("perchance Mestizo, Portuguese, of a Persian-Turkish mother in Libya born," T-A 37), an eccentric millionaire who spends his days looking for young men that might agree to have sex in exchange for money and who is currently in love with Ignacy, the teenage son of a Polish nobleman. Witold's first reaction is panic and a desire to escape ("I drew back as in that confusion and consternation of mine I knew not what he would and what [he] asks for, or perchance Lusts for," T-A, 37), but it quickly becomes too late for that, especially since other people have already acknowledged him as Gonzalo's companion, perhaps even his lover. This, to Witold's surprise and embarrassment, makes him immediately popular: in the men's toilets, his Polish compatriots enthusiastically congratulate Witold on his new relationship ("But that man sits on millions! You are not as mad as people say," T-A 44). Gonzalo, it should be noted, in spite of his bizarre lifestyle (and despite his wish to eliminate Tomasz, Ignacy's father), is portrayed as a positive figure. In contrast to most Argentinian elites, he is not a snob, his attitude toward Witold is fair and straightforward, and, quite importantly, he does not want to dominate or exploit his sexual partners. On the contrary, it is he who takes (and enjoys) the risk and discomfort of cruising alone on the streets of Buenos Aires:

> Now after another Brunet or a Blond, accosting, inquiring. Then [...] again onto a street to look for, walk, approach, ask now a Craftsman, now a Labourer or an Apprentice, or a Scullery Lad or a Soldier, or a Sailor. [...] If then he came by such a one and has settled on terms for ten, fifteen, or twenty Pesos, straightway to his lodging leads him; and there, having locked the door with a key, he his jacket, tie, trousers doffs, drops on the Floor, undresses down to his Shirt and the light dims, Perfume sprays. And here the Lad him in the jaw and to the Wardrobe to seize his linen or snatch his Cashes! Numb from a terrible fear Puto dares not cry out, allows him to take all and suffers his painful blows. From those Blows, Cuffs, his Heat even stronger! So after the Lad has left, he again into the street, blazing, Flaming, enraptured and likewise Terrified, Anguished, and on after Apprentices, young Craftsmen, Soldiers or Sailors; but whenever forth he steps, Back he steps for, although the lust great, the Fear greater than the lust.
>
> (T-A 37–38)

Gonzalo is to be seen as a synecdochical portrait of Argentinian *putos* (male homosexuals) of the 1940s, one of the very first in Argentinian literature.[18]

At the same time, in his figure, Gombrowicz also portrays his own homosexual experiences of Buenos Aires and its harbor neighborhood Retiro (in 1939 Argentina, homosexuals were still a target of various discriminatory laws).[19]

Despite his passions and obsessions, Gonzalo is also one of the very few down-to-earth figures throughout the entire novella. He represents not only "the external" perspective in the portrayal of the milieu of bumptious Polish emigrants, but also the more "universal" common sense, which becomes particularly visible when he has a conversation with Witold about beautiful Ignacy and the more abstract values (such as "the Fatherland") concerning which he has neither understanding nor interest. Witold reacts first with fear and indignation, yet later he cannot get Gonzalo's concept of "Filistria" out of his mind. Moreover, he himself starts to be interested in Ignacy (whom he usually calls "the Son"). In a moment of a great sadness and despair, Witold has a sudden need to see Ignacy; he sneaks to his house at night just to adore the sleeping teenager for a while. Interestingly, Gonzalo rather refrains from any direct seductive action toward Ignacy and instead asks his teenage servant Horatio to play sport with him (watching Ignacy and Horatio playing stickball also intensifies Witold's feelings). In other words, the erotic fascinations in *Trans-Atlantyk* have to be mediated by someone else (cf. the Girardian concept of mimetic desire).[20] However, the reader will not know whether Gonzalo's attempts prove successful, as the novella ends in a typically Gombrowiczian absurd and non-conclusive way, with Ignacy's outburst of laughter

Figure 3.3 Tango Between Men in Buenos Aires. Author unknown. Public Domain. Tango was danced by men due to the prevalence of male-only gatherings in port cities.

that sets off a general eruption of all-encompassing hilarity. (As Gombrowicz emphasized in a letter to Mariano Betelú in 1958, "a young man who is laughing is INVINCIBLE.")[21]

Less than a decade after *Trans-Atlantyk*, Gombrowicz wrote his next longer piece of prose in Argentina: the novel ***Pornografia*** (Polish: "pornography"), published in 1960. Contrary to *Trans-Atlantyk*, it did not evoke such emotional responses from ordinary readers; however, literary critics and reviewers received it with mixed feelings (one of them complained that "[t]he title appears to be a conscious overstatement").[22] Gombrowicz set his story in the circumstances of the Second World War in conquered Poland, in the year 1943. The reality of the Nazi German occupation in the Polish rural areas becomes a background for erotic intrigues arranged by two men: Witold (the narrator) and the mysterious Fryderyk. Witold falls in love in Karol, a teenager who works as a servant in the manor, and together with Fryderyk tries to manipulate the desires of Karol and Henia, the daughter of the landowner. The horror of the war is rather suggested than shown: instead of depicting Nazi atrocities, Gombrowicz makes scarce mention of such details as additional iron bars in windows, displaced persons on the road, and the clatter of railroads (a hint at transports to death camps?).[23] Moreover, he refrains from using the obvious terms that might suggest a military conflict; words such as "expulsion," "massacre," "camp," or the like are absent from the novel.[24] The annihilation of the Jews is summarized in one simple yet chilling remark: while describing the trip to the town of Ostrowiec, located relatively close to the camps of Majdanek, Sobibor, and Auschwitz-Birkenau, Witold notices: "Just one thing, an absence was palpable, namely, there were no Jews" (POR 70). *Pornografia*'s taciturn style of describing the German occupation was the reason why Czesław Miłosz—always skeptical of overemotional Polish war discourses—was very enthusiastic about the novel,[25] whereas the Polish critic of Jewish origin Artur Sandauer did not hide his indignation at the treatment of the period of Nazi terror as a setting for (homo)erotic interactions.[26] No less significantly, *Pornografia* is the first of Gombrowicz's longer pieces of prose that is entirely devoid of humor.

What appears instead of hilarity is a genuine lyricism. One of the pivotal moments of the novel is a scene in a provincial church, when Fryderyk (an atheist) tries to actively take part during a Catholic mass and behave like all the other people gathered there, but—at least in Witold's perception—all his efforts to adjust and follow the ceremony only deprive the mass of its actual meaning. The mass is "kill[ed] [like] a hen," becoming an empty ritual. Witold then experiences a paralyzing feeling of human desolation in the universe, a cosmic "severity and emptiness" (POR 22). But just after that, he notices Karol, the 16-year-old who works at Hipolit's manor, and his despair disappears immediately, replaced by an astonishment mixed with a genuine sensual delight, reverence, and fear. All of a sudden, the sanctity removed by Fryderyk is back; the notions such as "grace," "God," "significance," and "miracle" are no longer empty.

> I circled around like this, still flustered, hesitant … yet already deliciously permeated by a lithe subjugation that was captivating me—enchanting—charming—tempting and conquering me—it sparkled—and the contrast between that night's cosmic chill and the gushing spring of bliss was so immeasurable that I thought dimly—it's God, and a miracle! God and a miracle!
>
> What was it, though?
>
> It was … part of a cheek and the nape of a neck … it belonged to someone standing in front of us, in the crowd, a few steps away …
>
> Oh, I almost choked! It was …
>
> (a boy)
>
> (a boy)
>
> And realizing that it was just (a boy), I began to rapidly retreat from my ecstasy. Because in fact I barely saw him, just a little ordinary skin—on the back of the neck and on the cheek. Then he moved abruptly, and this movement, imperceptible, pierced me through and through, like an extraordinary attraction!
>
> And indeed (a boy).
>
> And nothing but (a boy).
>
> How embarrassing! An ordinary sixteen-year-old nape of a neck, with cropped hair, and the ordinary skin (of a boy), somewhat chapped, and (a youthful) position of the head—most ordinary—so what was the origin of my inner trembling? Oh … and now I saw the contour of the nose, the mouth, for he turned his face slightly to the left—there was nothing special, I saw in this slant the slanting face (of a boy)—an ordinary face! He was not a peasant. A student? An apprentice? An ordinary (young) face, untroubled, somewhat willful, friendly, meant for chewing pencils with his teeth, or for playing football, playing billiards, and the collar of the jacket was over the shirt collar, his nape was suntanned. Yet my heart was beating fast. And he exuded godliness, wonderfully enchanting and engaging as he was in the boundless emptiness of this night, he was a source of a breathing warmth and light. Grace. Unfathomable miracle: why did this insignificance become significant?
>
> (POR 22–24)

One can observe here a very striking resemblance to Thomas Mann's novella *Death in Venice* of 1912.[27] Mann's main hero, a middle-aged writer

Gustav Aschenbach, bored with life, takes a holiday in Venice, where he unexpectedly falls in love in a beautiful Polish youth, Tadzio, who, together with his family, is staying in the same hotel. For Aschenbach, observing Tadzio becomes the source of aesthetic and sensual pleasure and allows him to experience again true emotional involvement—the feeling that he had forgotten many years ago. Aschenbach's passion is the reason he does not leave Venice despite the outbreak of cholera which eventually kills him. Like the war in *Pornografia*, the epidemic in *Death in Venice* enriches the story with a motif of all-encompassing lethal danger, which in both cases leads to linking eroticism with death.[28] Gombrowicz leaves in his work a small, yet direct hint at Mann's novella, as Fryderyk mentions Venice twice, in two conversations.

Figure 3.4 Thomas Mann in Los Angeles (between 1925 and 1945). Los Angeles Daily News.

Pornografia also explores the crucial question of *Death in Venice*, namely, the epistemic dimension of erotic fascination. In both works, falling in love leads to the realization of one's own transience,[29] as well as the general "awfulness" of human bodies that are adult (POR 207), since the youth and beauty of Karol/Tadzio mercilessly expose Witold's/Aschenbach's advanced age and thus their bygone physical attractiveness. As Juan J. Saer notices, in Gombrowicz's world the process of aging is such a huge trauma that it could be compared to patricide in the works of Sophocles.[30]

Pornografia, mostly because of the figure of the mass-killer Fryderyk (whose name is the Polish version of "Friedrich"), is often described as a "Nietzschean" novel.[31] Indeed, in Gombrowicz's work aesthetics (beauty and charm) is meant to replace ethics (the "standardized" morals, but also compassion and sympathy), which bears a strong resemblance to Nietzschean positions expressed for instance in his *Genealogy of Morality*.[32] Witold's fascination with the beautiful young Karol deprives him of the ability to sympathize with two suffering adult men next to him: the lawyer Vaclav whose mother was murdered by her own servant and who is now afraid of being betrayed by his fiancée, and the Polish Home Army officer, Siemian, who experiences a serious mental breakdown. In Witold's eyes, they are grown men (and thus they are physically appalling); moreover, they are not ashamed to annoy him with their self-pity. Hence, in his opinion, his lack of any consideration is understandable and justified: "*All beauty was on the other, the young, side*" (POR 207, Gombrowicz's emphasis).

> Was he suffering? Suffering? Well, yes, he was suffering, but it was a pudgy kind of suffering—weary—balding. …
>
> The charm was on the other side. So I was "on the other side" too. Everything that came from there was—delightful and … skilled in enticement … endearing … Body.That bull, who was pretending to defend morality, was in reality bearing down on them with all his weight. Bearing down on them with his very self. He was inflicting on them that morality of his for no other reason than that it was his "own"—it carried more weight, was older, more developed … the morality of a grown man. Inflicting it by force!
>
> (POR 170)

In *Pornografia*, the charm of youth follows from its amorality, that is, its quasi-innocent being "beyond good and evil." When the question of a potential murder committed by a teenager arises, none of the adult novel protagonists is ready to consider such an act to be a real felony: the young age of the perpetrator deprives a crime of its "regular" weight, even if it was committed on purpose.[33] Witold's erotic fascination with Karol can be thus seen as tiredness with the general awfulness and "morality of a grown man" (POR 170) and longing for the beauty, charm, and amorality of the youth.

It is worth reading *Pornografia* and *Diary* in parallel. Particularly the fragments from the second half of his sixth decade (i.e. after 1956, when *Pornografia* was being written) provide much insight into the extent to which Gombrowicz was then preoccupied with the issues of youth, aging processes, carnal beauty, and erotic delight. Much attention is also devoted to the charm and enjoyment of life that is meant to characterize Argentinians, and the Argentinian youth in particular.[34]

> There, there at the table is the Argentina that has beguiled me—it is quiet but has the sound of great art [...]. Why am I not sitting over there with them? My place is over there! Next to the girl who is like a tremulous black and white bouquet, next to the young man who looks like Rudolph Valentino! ... Belleza!
>
> (D 379)

> Then suddenly I heard a fist pounding on the kitchen door, and Colimba walked in, dripping wet! [...] His face was rich with adventure, like a film, swinging acrobatically from seriousness to jest, from groan to joy, from poetry to rambunctiousness, from compassion to anger, his face immediately filled the whole room and I probably never had a stronger sense that the *potential of someone's joy is not inaccessible, that one can gain access to someone's joy, if it is young.* [...] Sometimes my hopelessness is visited by a spark of conviction, a completely palpable certainty that *salvation is not impossible.* This is exactly what I was feeling while [Colimba] prepared my food and opened the bottle he had brought.
>
> (D 389, Gombrowicz's emphasis)

In *Diary*, there are plethora of similarly passionate, almost poetic descriptions of adolescent Argentinians—how they smile, how they laugh, how they enjoy spending time together. (Even skeptical readers of Gombrowicz's writings, such as the Italian intellectual and film director Pier Paolo Pasolini, were deeply impressed by those parts of the book.)[35] This might raise some questions concerning a link between eroticization and exoticization,[36] but on the other hand, it also helps to notice how the issues of sensuality in Gombrowicz's work changed over the time spent in *la Patria*, especially as he became confronted with the realization of his own aging and progressively deteriorating health.

In the last literary writings of Gombrowicz, on can observe the return of some motifs that were characteristic of his prewar oeuvre. In the piece *Operetta* (1966), he again plays with the notion of sexual attraction and being good-looking, but this time an elegant appearance is contrasted not with ugliness, but with pure nudity. A dandy Count Charmant, the son of Prince Himalay, organizes an intrigue to seduce the young and naïve Albertine and to eventually "dress her [up]" (Charmant is a fashion lover). Yet his plan backfires: although Albertine's sexual drives become awakened, she is still not attracted by Charmant's stylish outfits and sophisticated manners. Instead, she suddenly starts to desire the state of pure nakedness. Throughout the greater part of the play, she remains in a state of half-sleep and lustfully whispers only one word: "nude" (*nagość*). By the same token, in Gombrowicz's last novel, *Cosmos* (1965), the motif of sexual interest in servants reappears: the main protagonist, Witold, is interested in certain Lena, yet at the same time cannot stop thinking of the handmaid Katasia and her "distortion of the upper lip" (COS 10). Moreover, the owner of the resort where Witold spends his holidays regard intercourse he once had with a kitchen maid as the most significant thing he has ever experienced ("My good sir! Once in my life I got lucky, and how! I carry this delight of mine within myself like the holiest sacrament. Once in my life!," COS 140). Both works, *Operetta* and *Cosmos*, link eroticism to the issue of nothingness and its various graduations and manifestations (transience, deterioration, and death), and thus reveal its intrinsically existential dimension.

Notes

1 Thompson, *Witold Gombrowicz*, 121.

2 My translation. Originally in Polish: *Co się zaś tyczy w szczególności czynnika seksualnego, przewaga jego wynika z ducha czasu, który, niestety coraz silniej akcentuje związek sfery płciowej ze sferą duchową*. Witold Gombrowicz in *Bakakaj*, 196.

3 This is perhaps the reason why Gombrowicz's short stories in particular (and not his later works) are investigated from a queer perspective; cf. the opening to the article: Warkocki, "A Queer Construction of Identity in the *Memoir of Stefan Czarniecki* by Witold Gombrowicz." Cf. Błażej Warkocki, "What Really Happened Aboard the Banbury? Reading Gombrowicz with Eve Kosofsky Sedgwick," in *Gombrowicz in Transnational Context: Translation, Affect, and Politics*, ed. Silvia G. Dapía, 126–141 (New York: Routledge, 2019). Cf. a fragment on sadomasochism: Piotr S. Rosół, "Becoming Gombrowicz: On the Way of Trans-Subjectivity and Trans-Modernity," in *Gombrowicz in Transnational Context: Translation, Affect, and Politics*, ed. Silvia G. Dapía, 115–125 (New York: Routledge, 2019), 120–122.

4 Dagmara Jaszewska, *Nasza niedojrzała kultura: Postmodernizm inspirowany Gombrowiczem* (Warszawa: Oficyna Naukowa, 2002), 194.

5 Suchanow, *Gombrowicz*, I 380–381, I 419–431.

6 Timothy Snyder, *Bloodlands: Europe Between Hitler and Stalin* (New York: Basic Books, 2010).

7 Suchanow, *Gombrowicz*, I 379–381.

8 Ricardo Piglia, "¿Existe La Novela Argentina? Borges Y Gombrowicz," *Espacios de crítica y producción*, no. 6 (1987), https://piglia.pubpub.org/pub/nx14ji96/release/1 (accessed January 18, 2022). Piglia's comparison should be seen as something of an exception, as the parallels between Gombrowicz and Borges are emphasized and analyzed mostly by non-Argentinian authors and scholars, for instance: Dieter Reichardt, "Gombrowicz vs. Borges," in *Gombrowicz in Europa: Deutsch-polnische Versuche einer kulturellen Verortung*, ed. Andreas Lawaty and Marek Zybura, 17–28 (Wiesbaden: Harrassowitz, 2006); George Gasyna, "Toward Heterotopia: The Case of *Trans-Atlantyk*," *Slavic Review* 68, no. 4 (2009): 912–919; Jerzy Jarzębski, *Gra w Gombrowicza* (Warszawa: Państwowy Instytut Wydawniczy, 1982), 425–426.

9 Juan J. Saer, "La perspectiva exterior: Gombrowicz en la Argentina," in *El concepto de ficción*, 17–29, Los tres mundos Ensayo (Buenos Aires: Seix Barral, 2004), cf. Suchanow, *Gombrowicz*, I 457–459.

10 Klementyna Suchanow, "El Caso Gombrowicz: La Traduccion De *Ferdydurke* De 1947," *Hispamerica* 36, no. 107 (2007); Suchanow, *Gombrowicz*, II 15–24.

11 Gombrowicz scrupulously noted the opinions of his Buenos Aires friends and acquaintances concerning the translation; most of them were positive. Witold Gombrowicz, *Kronika Ferdydurke [notes on the reception of Ferdydurke]*, 1947, GEN MSS 515 Box 12 f. 445, Witold Gombrowicz Archive, Beinecke Rare Book and Manuscript Library, Yale University.

12 Daniel Balderston, "Rex Café, Buenos Aires, 1947: On the Spanish Translation of Gombrowicz's *Ferdydurke*," *The Polish Review* 60, no. 2 (2015): 36.

13 Silvia G. Dapía, "'Living in Another Language': Witold Gombrowicz's Argentinean Experience," *Polish American Studies* 71, no. 2 (2014).

14 [Letters to "Kultura" concerning WG], 1951–1967, GEN MSS 515 Box 35 f. 1016, Witold Gombrowicz Archive, Beinecke Rare Book and Manuscript Library, Yale University.

15 Dietrich Scholze, "Zum Auto-Image des polnischen Exils: Gombrowicz und Polen in *Dziennik* und *Trans-Atlantyk*," in *Gombrowicz in Europa: Deutsch-polnische Versuche einer kulturellen Verortung*, ed. Andreas Lawaty and Marek Zybura, 68–78 (Wiesbaden: Harrassowitz, 2006).

16 The Polish laws that punished homosexuality were "inherited" from the German, Austrian, and Russian criminal codes that in the years 1918–1932 still simultaneously (!) functioned in the territories of the newly re-born Poland. The unification of the criminal code for Poland was not implemented until 1932, and homosexuality was then officially de-criminalized. Cf. Suchanow, *Gombrowicz*, I 279.

17 Cf. Miguel Grinberg, "Gombrowicz in Love," *Literatura na Świecie* 357, no. 4 (2001): 85. N.B. the polonaise is believed to originate from a peasant dance, the chodzony, which means "walking" or "pacing." See: Tomasz Nowak, *Polski, polonez, chodzony* (Roczyny: Fundacja "MEMO," 2018).

18 Carlos Gamerro, "The 'Puto' in Argentinian Literature," in *Gombrowicz in Transnational Context: Translation, Affect, and Politics*, ed. Silvia G. Dapía, 39–52 (New York: Routledge, 2019).

19 Suchanow, *Gombrowicz*, II 92–95.

20 René Girard, *Deceit, Desire, and the Novel: Self and Other in Literary Structure* (Baltimore: Johns Hopkins University Press, 1976). Ewa Thompson sees Girardian elements in the play *Operetta*: Thompson 1979, 144.

21 Juan C. Gómez, "Nowy przewodnik po Gombrowiczu," *Twórczość* 702, no. 5 (2004): 52. Gombrowicz's emphasis. Cf. Jan Błoński, *Forma, śmiech i rzeczy ostateczne: Studia o Gombrowiczu* (Kraków: Towarzystwo Autorów i Wydawców Prac Naukowych "Universitas," 2003); Daniel Pratt, "Affect and Youth: Reading Gombrowicz with Deleuze," in *Gombrowicz in Transnational Context: Translation, Affect, and Politics*, ed. Silvia G. Dapía, 142–153 (New York: Routledge, 2019), 143–145.

22 George J. Maciuszko, "[Review]," *Books Abroad* 35, no. 3 (1961): 303.

23 Agnieszka Dauksza, "Ciążąca (nie)obecność: Gombrowicz wobec wojny i Żydów," *Teksty Drugie*, no. 2 (2016).

24 Aleksandra Konarzewska, *Der Ausgang aus der Unmündigkeit: Sexualität, Kultivierung und Entzauberung der Welt in der Prosa von Stanisław Brzozowski und Witold Gombrowicz* (Frankfurt am Main: Peter Lang, 2020), 85–102.

25 As Miłosz writes, "[t]hose who claim that the background [to *Pornografia*] is 'unrealistic' (not the plot, it has a different aim) prove that they had not been in Poland during the war." Czesław Miłosz, "Who Is Gombrowicz?," *Performing*

Arts Journal 6, no. 3 (1982): 11. Cf. Witold Gombrowicz and Jerzy Giedroyc, *Listy 1950–1969*, ed. Andrzej S. Kowalczyk (Warszawa: Spółdzielnia Wydawnicza "Czytelnik," 2006), 437–438.

26 Charles Kraszewski, "Neither the Forest nor the Trees: Witold Gombrowicz's *Pornografia*: Failed Novel or Cynical Masterpiece?," *The Polish Review* 50, no. 1 (2005).

27 Thomas Mann, *Death in Venice*, with the assistance of Michael H. Heim ([s. l.]: Ecco, 2004). Cf. Patricia Merivale, "The Esthetics of Perversion: Gothic Artifice in Henry James and Witold Gombrowicz," *PMLA* 93, no. 5 (1978): 999; Jerzy Jarzębski, *Gra w Gombrowicza* (Warszawa: Państwowy Instytut Wydawniczy, 1982), 125–126.

28 I devoted a subchapter in my book to this question: Konarzewska, *Der Ausgang aus der Unmündigkeit*, 85–102. On other similarities between Mann and Gombrowicz, see: Alfred Gall, *Performativer Humanismus: Die Auseinandersetzung mit Philosophie in der literarischen Praxis von Witold Gombrowicz* (Dresden: Thelem, 2007), 277–281, 320–327.

29 Cf. Robert Boyers, "Aspects of the Perverse in Gombrowicz' *Pornografia*," *Salmagundi*, no. 17 (1971): 25.

30 Juan J. Saer in *El concepto de ficción*, 22; cf. Michal Oklot, "Gombrowicz's *Kronos*: The Pornography of Aging," *Slavonica* 19, no. 2 (2014): 109.

31 Thompson, *Witold Gombrowicz*, 138–145; Anna Tatarkiewicz, "Anty-wieszcz i jego prorok," *Więź*, VII–VIII (1972); Gall, *Performativer Humanismus*, 261–327; Michał Głowiński, *Gombrowicz i nadliteratura* (Kraków: Wydawnictwo Literackie, 2002), 104, 106–109.

32 Friedrich W. Nietzsche, *On the Genealogy of Morality*, ed. Keith Ansell-Pearson (Cambridge, New York: Cambridge University Press, 2007). See also: Janusz Margański, "Między powiastką a filozofią: O *Ferdydurke* Witolda Gombrowicza," *Pamiętnik Literacki*, no. 1 (2000): 130–131; Silvia G. Dapía, "The First Poststructuralist: Gombrowicz's Debt to Nietzsche," *The Polish Review* 54, no. 1 (2009).

33 Cf. Daniel Just, "The Difficult Childhood of an Adult: Aging and Maturity in Witold Gombrowicz's Pornografia," *Russian Literature* 116 (2020; Daniel Pratt, "Affect and Youth," in *Gombrowicz in Transnational Context*, 149, 151–152.

34 German Ritz, "Körper, Geschlecht und Gender im autobiographischen Projekt Witold Gombrowiczs," in *Gombrowicz in Europa: Deutsch-polnische Versuche einer kulturellen Verortung*, ed. Andreas Lawaty and Marek Zybura, 308–325 (Wiesbaden: Harrassowitz, 2006), 321–325.

35 Pier P. Pasolini, "Witold Gombrowicz, Diario 1957–61," in *Tutte le opere: Saggi sulla letteratura e sull'arte,* ed. Walter Siti and Silvia de Laude, 1712–7 2 (Milano: Mondadori, 1999).

36 Aleksander Fiut proposes considering Gombrowicz as a postcolonial writer, but the question of the eroticization of "exotic" bodies is not raised. Aleksander Fiut, "Gombrowicz the First Post-Colonialist?," *Russian Literature* 62, no. 4 (2007).

4 Self

It would be difficult to indicate any other author of the twentieth century who treated the question of human identity with the same subversive flair and insightful humor as Gombrowicz.[1] Particularly his magnum opus, *Diary* (1953–1969), delves into the multifaceted nature of the self, exploring the intricate relationships between his own entangled identities as a Pole, an émigré, and a writer. Gombrowicz posits that a serious writer must forge their own personality, and he argues that the experience of exile provides a heightened understanding of the artificiality of identity categories such as nationhood, political orientation, being an intellectual, and belonging to a certain literary milieu. Central to *Diary* is also the question of what it means to be a writer or artist, especially in an era of the simultaneous massification, professionalization, and intellectualization of culture.

In his youth, Gombrowicz was a prime example of a smart and yet very lazy student who managed to progress through all levels of his formal education thanks to a combination of intelligence, eloquence, financial support from his family, and a healthy dose of good fortune. After he completed his studies at the Faculty of Law at the University of Warsaw, his father provided him with the resources to spend an additional year in Paris as an auditor at the Institute of Advanced International Studies (*Institut des hautes études internationales,* EHEI). Gombrowicz recalls in *Polish Memories* that instead of attending lectures or immersing himself in the city's museums, galleries, and libraries, he spent his time meandering aimlessly through the Parisian streets. During this period, he was clarifying his outlook on the "West," and his own national identity, particularly regarding his belonging to a culture that, during the era of colonial empires and sharp distinctions between "centers" and "peripheries," could at best be considered semi-peripheral. For Gombrowicz, Poland and other Eastern and Central European states constituted "countries of degraded Form" (TES 66), whose inhabitants struggle to liberate themselves from an internalized stereotype as second-class Europeans—and usually fail, falling either into the intellectual trap of repetitive veneration of the Western ideal, or, even worse, into a naïve idolization of their own nation and its culture.[2] When decades later, in his *Testament*, Gombrowicz described his juvenile struggles with "the West," he pointed out the danger of oscillating

DOI: 10.4324/9781003183976-4

between these two extremes (as they both lead to artificiality and mannerism), and subtly alluded to Honoré Balzac's literary diptych *The Poor Relations* (*Les Parents pauvres,* 1846–1847):

> For a painter or a writer from the countries of degraded Form, from the frontier zones of Europe, the journey to Paris, Rome, or London adopted the proportions of an important problem. How was he to behave? How should he adapt himself? Calm respect and discretion? Cold politeness? Admiration? Humility? The shameless irony of the demi-barbarian? Familiarity? Premeditated simplicity? All those tactics only have one fault: they betray a violent inferiority complex. And unfortunately, this inferiority complex is incurable simply because it is not a complex, but the reality… the reality, I should add, of the poor relations (*rzeczywistość ubogich krewnych*).
>
> (TES 66)

The down-to-earth approach concerning one's national belonging is present in Gombrowicz's earliest works, in which he employs the aesthetics of the grotesque to ridicule the idealization of military violence and other elements of "patriotic" socialization in Poland,[3] particularly the school upbringing. In the short story "The Memoirs of Stefan Czarniecki," a primary school teacher who harbors disdain for the main protagonist's half-Jewish heritage, instructs his pupils that "[a]s concerns the number of geniuses, especially precursors, we [the Poles] have as many of them as the whole of Europe combined. […] Our language is a hundred times richer than French, which is supposedly the most perfect tongue. What does the Frenchman have? *Petit, petiot, très petit at the most.* But what riches we have: small, little, titchy, tiny, teeny, teeny-weeny, teensy-weensy, and so on" (BAC 22–23). Correspondingly, in *Ferdydurke*, Gombrowicz's prewar novel, a Polish language teacher with the telling nickname Ashface (*Bladaczka*) attempts to persuade his disinterested students that the poetry of the Romantic author Juliusz Słowacki (1809–1849) deserves absolute "admiration and love" solely because "Słowacki was a great poet" (FER 42). (Similar to other nations where literature contributed to national awakenings, Romantic poetry in Poland holds the status of a national treasure and, therefore, knowledge and admiration of it is deemed a constituent element of Polish patriotism).[4] The truly hilarious fragment of *Ferdydurke* in which a wretched pedagogue repeats like a broken street organ commonplace banalities on Polish literature is one of the most recognizable passages in the novel, and indeed, in Gombrowicz's entire oeuvre.[5]

> "Hmm… hmm… Well then, why does Słowacki inspire our love and admiration? Why do we weep with the poet when we hear the Aeolian strings of his poem *In Switzerland*? Or, why are we swept away when we hear the heroic and stalwart verses of the *Spirit King*? And why can't we tear ourselves from the wonders and magic of *Balladyna*, why do the wails of *Lilla Weneda*

> tear our hearts to pieces? And why are we so willing to rush and speed to the rescue of the helpless king? Hmm… why? Because, gentlemen, Słowacki—oh, what a great poet he was! Walkiewicz! Why? Repeat why, Walkiewicz. Why the admiration and love, why do we cry, why the rapture, why the heartbreak, why do we rush and speed? Why, Walkiewicz, why? [...] And why do we love him? Because he was a great poet. A great poet he was indeed! You laggards, you ignoramuses, I'm trying to be calm and collected as I tell you this, get it into your thick heads—so, I repeat once more, gentlemen: a great poet, Juliusz Słowacki, a great poet, we love Juliusz Słowacki and admire his poetry because he was a great poet. Please make note of the following homework assignment: 'What is the immortal beauty which abides in the poetry of Juliusz Słowacki and evokes our admiration?'"
>
> (FER 41–42)

As can be seen, Gombrowicz's prewar struggles with Polish identity were not particularly sharp. He primarily poked fun at pompous and school-like discourses on nationhood and the naïve veneration of "our great people" from a common-sense perspective. This kind of critique, however, was not uncommon in Poland at the time, largely thanks to authors such as Antoni Słonimski and Tadeusz Boy-Żeleński (see Chapter 2). Although their voices were not in the majority, they had a real influence on the liberal-progressive intelligentsia in prewar Poland, and clearly inspired Gombrowicz as well. Boy-Żeleński analyzed the works of Polish Romantic authors, particularly Adam Mickiewicz, from a non-scholarly and purposefully down-to-earth perspective. In 1928, he half-ironically demanded that all monuments to Mickiewicz be destroyed as a necessary step that would enable Polish readers to eventually start treating Mickiewicz's oeuvres as *literature* and not as a kind of national Holy Scripture.[6]

About two decades later, a similarly joyful-blasphemous idea appears in Gombrowicz's novella *Trans-Atlantyk* (1953), in which the eccentric Argentinian millionaire Gonzalo advises the main character to forget his Polish identity, as "being a Pole" evidently prevents him from enjoying life (the novella is set in September 1939, at the outbreak of the Second World War, which makes Gonzalo's proposal even more frivolous). Gonzalo represents not only an external perspective on the portrayal of the milieu of Polish war emigrants in Buenos Aires but also common sense and pragmatism charmingly mixed with lasciviousness.[7] In a conversation about the fatherland and "Polishness," Gonzalo introduces the notion of the *Filistria* (*Synczyzna*, literally "a Sonland") and points out that abandoning "the Father" is the first step toward experiencing genuine carnal satisfaction:

> Exclaimed he: "But wherefore need you be a Pole?" Further says he: "Has the lot of the Poles up to now been so delightful? Has not your Polishness become loathsome to you? Have you not had your fill of Sorrow? Your fill of Soreness, Sadness? And today they are flaying your skins again!

> And you so insist on staying in that skin of yours? Would you not become something Else, something New? Would you have all these Boys of yours but just repeat everything forever after Fathers? Oh, release Boys from the paternal cage. Let them veer off the path, let them peer into the Unknown! [...] Gee-up, go! Give free rein to those Boys of yours, let them Gallop, let them Run, let them Bolt and be Carried away!"
>
> Thereupon I cried: "Be still! Cease that Importuning of yours as 'tis impossible for me to be against the Father and the land of our fathers, against Pater and Patria, and what's more, in a moment such as the present!"
>
> Mutters he: "To the Devil with Pater and Patria! The Son, the son's the thing, oh, indeed! But wherefore need you Patria? Is not Filistria better? You exchange Patria for Filistria and then you'll see!"
>
> (T-A 56–57)

Given that the postwar trauma was still very present in 1953, it is unsurprising that Gombrowicz's frolicsome wordplay on "Patria" and "Filistria" caused indignation among many Polish readers (see Chapter 3). However, *Trans-Atlantyk* already announces new tones in discussing the issue of nationality as a part of one's identity and individuality, tones that Gombrowicz develops in his monumental ***Diary*** (*Dzienník*).

Figure 4.1 *Polish Hamlet* (1903). Author: Jacek Malczewski. Public Domain. Malczewski's painting depicts the dilemma of Polish national identity during a turbulent historical period.

Diary exists in its current form thanks to Jerzy Giedroyc (1906–2000), the head of the Polish exile monthly *Kultura* (Culture). Giedroyc was a prominent political journalist, editor, and public intellectual who, in the aftermath of World War II, founded the influential journals *Kultura* and *Zeszyty Historyczne* (Historical Notebooks), as well as the publishing house Instytut Literacki. These publications provided a vital platform for critical thinking and discussion among exiled Polish intellectuals, and played a significant role in shaping Polish postwar culture and politics, both among exiles and, a few decades later, among anticommunist dissidents too. Notable authors published in Giedroyc's media included the most prominent European writers, poets, and thinkers of the postwar period, such as George Orwell (1903–1950), Milovan Đilas (1911–1995), Czesław Miłosz (1911–2004), Emil Cioran (1911–1995), Gustaw Herling-Grudziński (1919–2000), and Albert Camus (1913–1960). *Kultura*, *Zeszyty Historyczne*, and Instytut Literacki were known for their openness and pluralism, critique of totalitarian ideologies (particularly Soviet Communism), and equal interest in contemporary intellectual trends and the recent history of Eastern and Central Europe. One of Giedroyc's key aims was to promote a democratic and pluralistic vision for Poland's future, which emphasized the importance of a positive program that would facilitate reconciliation and cooperation between Poland and its neighboring countries, particularly Ukraine, Belarus, and Lithuania (then parts of the Soviet Union). Giedroyc launched, for instance, the initiative to publish in Instytut Literacki an anthology of works by Ukrainian modernist authors who were persecuted and exterminated during the Great Purge in the Soviet Union. The monumental volume *The Executed Renaissance: An Anthology 1917–1933* was compiled by the Ukrainian literary critic and scholar Yurii Lavrinenko (1915–1987), who was himself in exile in the United States.[8]

As a reader, Giedroyc was impressed not only by Gombrowicz's *Trans-Atlantyk*, but also by his insightful mini-essays on literature. In the spring of 1953, he encouraged Gombrowicz to publish similar pieces more often and suggested the form of a literary diary.[9] Gombrowicz quickly agreed to this proposal, and the same year, "Fragments from a Diary" (*Fragmenty z dziennika*) began appearing regularly in *Kultura*. It was initially meant to be an experiment allowing the author to mix freely elements of an essay, column, reportage, memoirs, pamphlet, and literary criticism.[10] Gombrowicz treated the *Diary* from the very outset as a genuinely literary project that would accompany him to the end of his life.[11] The three volumes of the *Diary* were published in 1957 (*Dziennik 1953–1956*), 1962 (*Dziennik 1957–1961*), and 1966 (*Dziennik 1961–1966*, which also includes the play *Operetta*). The newer editions of the *Diary* usually also include the later *Fragments...* that Gombrowicz wrote between 1966 and 1969, shortly before his death.

Gombrowicz's *Diary* is often considered his most significant work. Its form is to be seen as a contemporary *silva rerum* (*forest of things*), a nonfictional genre that was popular in seventeenth- and eighteenth-century Poland, in which collected content was arranged according to the personal preferences of the author rather than linear chronology and factual accuracy.[12] *Diary* has been compared, not without good reason, to the works of Friedrich Nietzsche, Francois Rabelais, and Michel de Montaigne, all of whom are renowned for their marvelous style and individualistic, unconventional perspectives.[13] Additionally, one can see similarities to Wittgenstein's succinct and yet persuasive writing.[14] In *Diary*, Gombrowicz manages to turn his objective disadvantages as an exile writer from an unknown country into one of his biggest assets. His ideological indecisiveness and rootlessness, together with his wariness of literary circles in Europe, allowed him to adopt an outsider's perspective and enjoy genuine intellectual freedom.[15] "Only he who knows how to reach deeper, beyond the homeland, only he for whom the homeland is but one of the revelations in an eternal and universal life, will not be incited to anarchy by the loss of his homeland," he wrote in 1952 in a short commentary comment on Emil Cioran (1911–1995), which was later included in the first volume of the *Diary* (D 50).[16] According to Gombrowicz, a serious writer is recognized by their aloofness toward any "homeland, ideology, politics, group, program, faith, milieu" (D 50), and the experience of exile gives them a better understanding of the artificiality of such categories. Therefore, a truly eminent and mature author will never be incapacitated by losing (or loosening) their ties with their native countries, languages, institutions, ideologies, and literary cliques.

What it means in practice is shown by Gombrowicz in the very first passages of the book. He briefly summarizes an article from an émigré Polish journal whose author maintains that Polish literature is not peripheral, and some important Polish writers, such as Adam Mickiewicz, deserve to be put in the same category as "Dante, Racine, and Shakespeare" (D 5). The only reason why this is not the case, according to the quoted author, is the lack of good translation and promotion of Polish literature. Gombrowicz contrasts this opinion with his own approach, which is entirely different. He argues that for an independent and sophisticated mind, there is always something awkward in praising one's own nation and demanding global recognition for its writers and artists, even though they might indeed have deserved more international appreciation. Such behavior immediately creates the impression of being an awkward "poor wretch who claims that his grandmother had a large estate and traveled to Paris" (D 7). The opening sections of the *Diary* further develop into a bitterly disillusioned and yet not humorless philippic against treating actual war trauma as an excuse for repeating the worn-out set of platitudes about one's own history and culture.[17] While the effects of war and totalitarian rule can be profound and long-lasting, argues Gombrowicz, it is not appropriate to use these traumata as justification for actions that would otherwise be considered deeply embarrassing and pathetic. As he brilliantly demonstrates, mixing self-pity with pompousness never leads to good results:

> [In Argentina,] I once happened to take part in a meeting devoted to yet another mutual Polish cheering up and support session, when, after having

> sung the [patriotic song] *Rota* and having danced the *Krakowiaczek*, everyone settled down to listen to the speaker, who extolled the nation because "we produced Chopin," "we have Curie-Skłodowska, Wawel, Słowacki, Mickiewicz," and because we also figured as a bulwark of Christianity and our Third of May Constitution was really quite progressive… The man explained to himself and to his audience that we are a great nation. […] I felt this ritual as if it were born of hell, this national Mass became something satanically sneering and maliciously grotesque. For they, in elevating Mickiewicz, were denigrating themselves and with their praise of Chopin showed that they had not yet sufficiently matured to appreciate him and that by basking in their own culture, they were simply baring their primitiveness.
>
> Geniuses! The devil takes those geniuses! I felt like saying to those gathered: Who cares about Mickiewicz? You are more important to me than Mickiewicz! And neither I nor anyone else will be judging the Polish nation according to Mickiewicz or Chopin, but according to that which goes on and which is said here in this hall. You could be a nation so devoid of greatness that your greatest artist might be Tetmajer or Konopnicka, yet if you talked about them with the ease of people *spiritually* liberated, with the proportion and sobriety of a mature people, or if your words could encompass the horizon of not some poor backwater but the world… then even Tetmajer would be cause for pride. But as things stand, Chopin and Mickiewicz serve only to emphasize your own narrow-mindedness […]. You are the poor relations of the world who try to impress themselves and others.
>
> (D 6–7)

Taking into account that after the Second World War and in the early 1950s, Polish people were still persecuted, jailed, and executed by the Stalinist regime ruled from Moscow, and that many of them had vivid memories of how their culture was targeted for annihilation (during the Nazi occupation of Poland, it was forbidden to play Chopin's music, monuments to Mickiewicz were destroyed or removed, and Poles were denied higher education),[18] it is not surprising that Gombrowicz's acerbic reasonableness was considered snide and condescending. To preempt likely critical responses, Gombrowicz includes in the first parts of the *Diary* some fragments of his correspondence with Czesław Miłosz,[19] who always despised Polish nationalism and respected how Gombrowicz managed to expose many pseudo-patriotic bromides. But at the same time, as someone who lived through the Second World War in Warsaw, Miłosz had firsthand knowledge of the atrocities committed during the German occupation in Poland; his judgment after 1945 was thus more cautious and balanced. In Miłosz's view, in *Trans-Atlantyk* Gombrowicz went too far in his critiques and parodies of Polish people and their mindsets, as he derided those who had recently experienced enough suffering due to historical and political events.

Miłosz's comments bear much resemblance in this respect to the remarks made by Gershom Scholem (1897–1982) exactly a decade later on Hannah Arendt's (1906–1975) book *Eichmann in Jerusalem* (1963). In a letter to Arendt, Scholem criticized her overly reserved attitude toward the Jewish people and her "flippancy" in describing the Shoah.[20] Arendt responded with a plea for unruffled independence of thought and judgment, emphasizing her deep mistrust of any group loyalties.[21] Gombrowicz's reply to Miłosz was very Arendtian (or, considering the chronology, Arendt's reply was very Gombrowiczian). The novella *Trans-Atlantyk* was meant to be an artistic creation of a free, independent spirit, and the focus on Polish affairs was intended to serve as a point of departure for a much more interesting question, namely, "a revision of the modern man in relation to form which is not a result of him but which is formed 'between' people" (D 19).[22] In another part of the *Diary*, Gombrowicz remarks that Miłosz is too considerate toward the victims of twentieth-century totalitarianisms and that a true artist should be able to refrain from such sentiments. As he put it:

> No, Miłosz, no history will replace your own personal consciousness, maturity, depth. Nothing will absolve you of yourself. If you personally are important, then even if you live in the most conservative place on the face of the globe, your testimony about life will be important. No historical steamroller will squeeze important words out of an immature people.
>
> (D 71)[23]

Throughout the *Diary*, Gombrowicz remains wary of any identity category and develops precisely this thought: the artificiality and yet the obviousness of national identity make it easier to understand and describe the more universal mechanisms of how one's self-concept is forged. The skeptical approach toward the category of the nation is thus a synecdochical element of Gombrowicz's suspicious attitude toward any kind of Form (with a capital F) that drives an individual to conceive of the world and behave in a particular way—and yet cannot be easily discarded. In the words of Jaroslaw Anders, "Form is often ridiculous and awkward. More importantly, however, it is the only thing modern man can hold on to when describing his identity."[24] From that point of view, one can see *Diary* as a theoretical continuation of the novel *Ferdydurke* that ends with the conclusion that "there is no escape from the mug, other than into another mug" (FER 281). This pessimistic conviction explains Gombrowicz's skeptical objections to the bare possibility of true cosmopolitanism, at least in his case. As he humorously put it in 1958, his focus on the question of "being a Pole" results from the lack of ability and motivation to ruminate on the question of other nationalities with a similar passion and wit and is also a statement against following whatever intellectual snobbery is currently in fashion ("I am sick of ideas that tell me to concern myself with China—I have not seen China, I don't know China, I haven't been there!," D 350).

From the perspective of the philosophy of Form, not only national identity is to be viewed with suspicion. To gain insight into the mechanisms involved in the formation of one's self-concept, Gombrowicz reflects extensively on the issue of a writer or artist's professional identity, particularly the question of what it means to be a writer or artist in an age when culture has become part of the industry. Interestingly, in most of his fictional works, Gombrowicz shows little interest in this matter. In his prose and drama plays, it seems to be intentionally avoided: even if certain characters have artistic ambitions (like Fryderyk in *Pornografia*), their aspirations only indirectly influence the main plot of those works. Furthermore, the age of mechanical reproduction of culture is presented from the layperson's perspective, whether it be an aspiring young man whose literary debut book was misunderstood by the critics (Joey in *Ferdydurke*) or a lay consumer who feels overwhelmed by the masses of contemporary cultural production (Gonzalo in *Trans-Atlantyk*). In *Trans-Atlantyk*, the issue is taken to the absurd, as Gonzalo, a millionaire, owns so many books that he hires professional readers to read them, as the constantly growing numbers of literary works in his library are beyond the capacity of any single individual.[25]

> "The library," says Gonzalo, "the library, what trouble I have with it! God's curse, for these are the most precious, the most esteemed Works of geniuses, of the leading minds of Mankind only, but what, lookye, if they Bite each other, Bite, and also Cheapen from their own superabundance for there are Too Many, Too Many, and every day new ones arrive and no one can read through since too many, oh, too Many! Ergo I, lookye, the Readers hired and pay them handsomely, as I am ashamed that all this lies Unread, but Too many; they cannot read through, even though with no break all day they read."
>
> (T-A 82)

Gonzalo's practical concern ("Too Many, Too Many") is one of many reflections on culture found in *Diary*, where Gombrowicz sheds new light on issues characteristic of the twentieth-century philosophy of culture and where the question of the massification of culture and its impact on the individual constitute the leitmotifs of the entire work. The reader can easily recognize the questions discussed by thinkers such as Walter Benjamin, José Ortega y Gasset, Theodor W. Adorno, Max Horkheimer, and Pierre Bourdieu: the massification and industrialization of culture, distinction mechanisms, taste, and snobbery.[26] However, contrary to them, Gombrowicz's tone in *Diary* remains feuilletonistically flippant, as if mere stylistic brilliance, cleverness, and a common-sense perspective were meant to guarantee discernment and

Figure 4.2 Newspaper stand in Buenos Aires (1956). Author: Grete Stern. Public Domain.

insightfulness. The wit and intellectual distance are achieved mostly through astute observations on Gombrowicz's own milieu (or on milieus that he deliberately tried to avoid).

Gombrowicz almost certainly did not know Walter Benjamin's seminal essay *The Work of Art in the Age of Mechanical Reproduction* (1935), but he would probably agree with one of its main theses, namely, that the value of the "genuine" work of art has its foundation in a ritual. In the modern world, where art is secularized (unlike previous epochs, in which art played an important role in religious practices), the notion of "authenticity" replaces the cult value, which has an impact on secular rituals of art worship.[27] In Gombrowicz's *Diary*, one can find analogous thoughts, but expressed in a provocatively naïve way:

> Why is this original [painting] worth ten million and its copy (even though it is so perfect that it makes the identical artistic impression) worth only ten thousand? Why is there a pious crowd that gathers before the original,

> but no one admires the copy? That painting supplied divine emotions as long as it was considered to be a "work of Leonardo," but today no one will look at it, because a paint analysis has shown that it is the work of an apprentice.
>
> (D 29)

Similar to the Spanish philosopher of culture José Ortega y Gasset (1883–1955), Gombrowicz considers quantity to be at odds with quality. This is because any cultural qualification in music, literature, and fine arts requires time, effort, and sometimes even a particular gift or talent (like musical hearing), and therefore it is rare. Additionally, "the most esteemed Works of geniuses" (to use Gonzalo's wording), in order to be fully understood and enjoyed, demand from a reader or listener a certain devotion and undisturbed focus. For an average consumer, who is ceaselessly attracted to newly produced books, paintings, films, and other cultural goods, such a focus is an unattainable extravagance. Consequently, in most cases, one has to rely on opinions that circulate in their social bubbles and milieus. As no one has enough capacity to ruminate deeply on each art exhibition, newly published book, or theater performance, it leads to a situation where one venerates almost solely those authors and artists who are already venerated, that is, praised in "cultural" media by other "cultural" people. This, in itself, is not a bad phenomenon (as it is how literary and artistic abilities and education are spread), but in Gombrowicz's eyes not recognizing such a simple dependency leads to an annoying pretentiousness (D 39–41). How many attendees of a philharmonic concert can understand and contextualize music well enough to state if the performance was really as magnificent as they expected? So why, after the concert, asks Gombrowicz, do they all behave as if they were music experts and feel obliged to formulate clever opinions that are in the best case just recycled statements of other snobs? Wouldn't it be easier for everyone if one admitted that a visit to a concert hall is a purely social event during which the music performed plays a much less important role than the exchange of courtesies and salon gossip during the intermission?

Puzzlingly, the twentieth-century democratization of culture turns out to be a false promise, as massification leads to a situation where the distinction between over-intellectualized "connoisseurs" (critics, scholars, journalists, columnists, reviewers) and "amateurs" ("average" consumers of culture) becomes ossified, and more and more importance is attached to the former group. In Gombrowicz's eyes, such a state is not only unnatural but also highly troublesome for those authors (writers, artists, musicians) who would prefer to respond spontaneously to fleeting moments of artistic inspiration instead of tediously crystallizing "the actual message" of their works so that they can cater to the preferences of a few snobs who hold editorial positions in cultural magazines. This conviction results from strong anthropological assumptions: in Gombrowicz's universe, as Włodzimierz Bolecki put it, a human being "is not *homo doctus* but *homo ludens*; culture is not an area of knowledge but one of life and play."[28] The contemporary over-intellectualization of the cultural discourse and the overproduction of different "-isms" in analyses of literary works have a detrimental effect on the creative self of contemporary artists and writers and thus remain in *Diary* as an object of constant critique—sometimes expressed humorously, sometimes bitterly, sometimes reflectively.

> And today's artist, who has lost his instinct, is especially sensitive to arguments. This is what has been happening to him since the time when, intimidated by science, he drowned his temperament in intellect and began to smell the flowers not with his nose but with his soul. What should one demand from the naive but noble-minded scruples of those "working on themselves," perfecting themselves, analyzing, constructing their morality, trembling in the face of their responsibilities, suffering for all of humanity, those researchers, teachers, leaders, judges, inspectors, engineers of souls, finally martyrs, sometimes even saints—but not dancers, singers.... Art fried up in laboratories... but what should one demand from these fried eggs, what can this omelet possibly resist?
>
> (D 502)

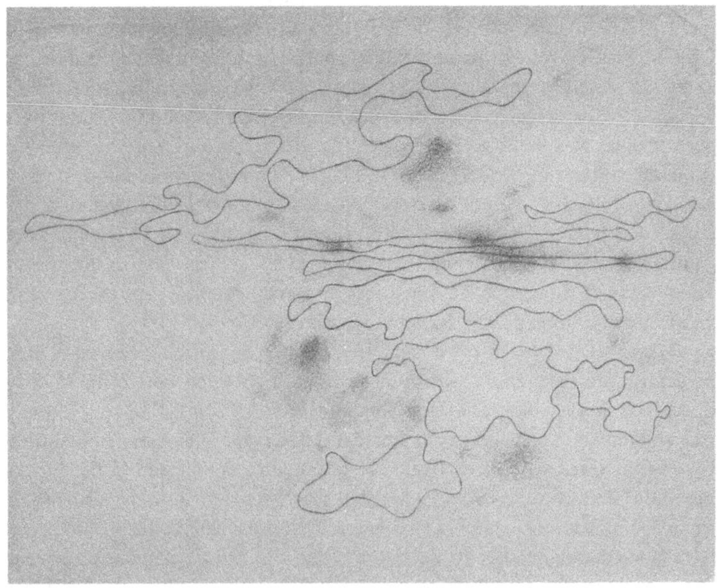

Figure 4.3 *Pejzaż morski* (1939). Author: Władysław Strzemiński. Public Domain. Władysław Strzemiński (1893–1952) was a prominent Polish avant-garde artist and a key figure in the constructivist movement.

Notes

1 Kazimiera Szczuka, "Gombrowicz subwersywny," *Teksty Drugie* 58, no. 5 (1999).
2 Cf. Błoński, *Forma, śmiech i rzeczy ostateczne*, 240–244.
3 Jativa, "Form and Power."
4 As Jaroslaw Anders put it, "East European writers [...] have been often cast by history in the role, to paraphrase Shelley, of moral legislators of their people. They were supposed to stand like immovable rocks in the turbulent sea of their region's fate." Jaroslaw Anders, *Between Fire and Sleep: Essays on Modern Polish Literature* (New Haven: Yale University Press, 2009), 28. To understand better the Polish veneration of a *wieszcz* (a Romantic poet and a patriotic prophet), suffice it to say that two of them, Adam Mickiewicz (1798–1855) and Juliusz Słowacki, are buried together with the Polish kings in Wawel Castle in Cracow.
5 That Gombrowicz's attitude to Słowacki's work was in fact quite positive, see: Włodzimierz Bolecki, "Słowacki Gombrowicza," *Teksty Drugie* 121–122, 1–2 (2007). See also: Beth Holmgren, "Witold Gombrowicz Within the Wieszcz Tradition," *The Slavic and East European Journal* 33, no. 4 (1989).
6 Tatarkiewicz, "Anty-wieszcz i jego prorok." Boy-Żeleński proposed "[t]ear[ing] down all the monuments to Mickiewicz, cast a huge cannon from them and scoop a number of his commentators into it." Tadeusz Boy-Żeleński, "Mickiewicz a my," in *Reflektorem w mrok: Wybór publicystyki*, ed. Andrzej Z. Makowiecki, 459–484 (Warszawa: Państwowy Instytut Wydawniczy, 1985), 483–484.
7 Cf. Jaroslaw Anders's opinion of that "at the time *Trans-Atlantyk* was written Gombrowicz was even more aware that "nations die" when Form becomes a unifying principle in a mass society." Anders, *Between Fire and Sleep*, 41.
8 The title *The Executed Renaissance* was also coined by Giedroyc. Yurii Lavrinenko, ed., *Rozstriliane Vidrodzhennia: Antolohiia 1917–1933: Poeziia—Proza—Drama—Esei*, Biblioteka "Kultury" XXXVII (Paryż: Instytut Literacki, 1959), https://staticnowyportal.kulturaparyska.com/attachments/51/58/1c83543de7383cf82472ec5ea5a3d67a0f7be0f9.pdf (accessed March 1, 2023).
9 Giedroyc put this explicitly in a letter of April 13, 1953: "The form of *Fragments from a Diary* is very good, and I would encourage you to continue it." Gombrowicz and Giedroyc, *Listy 1950–1969*, 111.
10 According to Paweł Rodak, thanks to its provocative style, *Dziennik* is to be seen as an *interactive* literary form, as it indeed evoked differentiated and expressive reactions in *Kultura* readers. Paweł Rodak, "Dziennik Gombrowicza: Między mową, pismem i drukiem (Wstępne rozpoznanie)," *Przegląd Filozoficzno-Literacki* 10, no. 4 (2001): 94.
11 However, it was also Giedroyc's idea to publish *Diary* as a book. Gombrowicz and Giedroyc, *Listy 1950–1969*, 114.
12 Ryszard Nycz, *Sylwy współczesne* (Kraków: Towarzystwo Autorów i Wydawców Prac Naukowych Universitas, 1996), 84–112.
13 Wojciech Karpiński, "Głos Gombrowicza," in *Książki zbójeckie*, 141–59 (Warszawa: Zeszyty Literackie, 2009), 155. Bronisław Łagowski, "Inny Gombrowicz," in *Gombrowicz filozof*, ed. Francesco M. Cataluccio and Jerzy Illg, 168–176 (Kraków: Społeczny Instytut Wydawniczy Znak, 1991), 170–171; Gall, *Performativer Humanismus*, 434–458; Jarzębski, *Gra w Gombrowicza*, 367–368.
14 Janusz Margański, "Filozof Gombrowicz," *Teksty Drugie* 11, no. 5 (1991): 114.
15 Klara Lutsky speaks of "freedom from all social and cultural pressures." Klara Lutsky, "Living on the Margins and Loving It: Gombrowicz and Exile," in *Literature in Exile of East and Central Europe*, ed. Agnieszka Gutthy, 73–87 (New York: Peter Lang, 2009), 79.
16 Witold Gombrowicz, "Komentarz," in *Polemiki i dyskusje*, ed. Włodzimierz Bolecki, Varia 2 (Kraków: Wydawnictwo Literackie, 2004).

17 Dietrich Scholze, "Zum Auto-Image des polnischen Exils," in *Gombrowicz in Europa.*

18 Katarzyna Naliwajek, "Nazi Musical Imperialism in Occupied Poland," in *The Routledge Handbook to Music under German Occupation, 1938–1945: Propaganda, Myth and Reality*, ed. David Fanning and Erik Levi, Routledge Handbooks Online (Abingdon: Routledge, 2019), https://www.routledgehandbooks.com/doi/10.4324/9781315230610-4.

19 Witold Gombrowicz, [Letters to Czeslaw Milosz from Witold Gombrowicz], 1954–1969, GEN MSS 661 Box 21 f. 350, Czesław Miłosz Papers, Beinecke Rare Book and Manuscript Library, Yale University.

20 Gershom Scholem, "[Letter 132]," in *The Correspondence of Hannah Arendt and Gershom Scholem*, ed. Marie L. Knott and Anthony David (Chicago: University of Chicago Press, 2017). Cf. Gershom Scholem, "[Letter 135]," in *The Correspondence of Hannah Arendt and Gershom Scholem*, ed. Marie L. Knott and Anthony David, 211–214 (Chicago: University of Chicago Press, 2017).

21 Hannah Arendt, "[Letter 133]," in *The Correspondence of Hannah Arendt and Gershom Scholem*, ed. Marie L. Knott and Anthony David, 205–210 (University of Chicago Press, 2017).

22 Daniel Pratt, "Narrative and Form: Gombrowicz and the Narrative Conception of Personal Identity," *The Polish Review* 60, no. 2 (2015): 14–15.

23 Cf. Witold Gombrowicz and Czesław Miłosz, *Konfrontacje*, ed. Michał Szymański and Barbara Toruńczyk (Warszawa: Zeszyty Literackie, 2015).

24 Anders, *Between Fire and Sleep*, 35.

25 George Gasyna, "Toward Heterotopia: The Case of "Trans-Atlantyk," *Slavic Review* 68, no. 4 (2009): 917–919.

26 Błoński, *Forma, śmiech i rzeczy ostateczne*, 230–231.

27 Walter Benjamin, *Das Kunstwerk im Zeitalter seiner technischen Reproduzierbarkeit* (Frankfurt am Main: Suhrkamp, 2010), 22.

28 Włodzimierz Bolecki, "Gombrowicz and Science," *Russian Literature* 62, no. 4 (2007): 397. Cf. Błoński, *Forma, śmiech i rzeczy ostateczne*, 239.

5 Intersubjectivity

"Intersubjectivity" is a term referring to the dynamic interaction between individuals and their subjective experiences when two or more individuals engage in communication. Today, this concept is central to various disciplines (such as psychology, sociology, anthropology), but it was initially forged by German philosopher Edmund Husserl (1859–1938), the key representative of the philosophical current known as phenomenology. Phenomenology, in its essence, is a radical attempt to shift the emphasis of philosophical inquiry into the world. According to Husserl, intersubjectivity is a fundamental feature of experience (as we always encounter others as intentional beings with their own thoughts, feelings, and perceptions), which means that human perception of the world is not just individual, but also social, mediated by other beings and their insight. The intersubjective experience is thus indispensable to grasping the objective world.[1] Later, the concept of intersubjectivity was further developed by existentialist philosophers such as Martin Heidegger (1889–1976), Jean-Paul Sartre (1905–1980), and Albert Camus (1913–1960), all of whom built upon Husserl's ideas to explore the ways in which people interact and create shared meanings. Sartre and Camus, who were also active as writers and dramaturgs, underscored the paramount importance of the individual's subjective experience and the relationships between individuals in their literary works as well. In Poland, by contrast, Husserl's direct disciple and former doctoral student Roman Ingarden successfully combined phenomenology with aesthetics and literary theory.[2]

Recalling the concept of intersubjectivity allows one to conceive of further aspects of one of Gombrowicz's key concepts: Form. While Gombrowicz did not have any formal or academic philosophical training, he knew and appreciated phenomenology and considered Husserl's "phenomenological reduction" to be a philosophical method that makes possible "the purification and classification of the phenomena of our consciousness" (GP 48). Gombrowicz's works thus grapple with phenomenology-inspired questions, the issue of intersubjectivity/Form being a good example. In his prose and drama, he probes Form as an intricate interplay between the individual and the collective, the subjective and the objective, and the dialectical tension between personal

DOI: 10.4324/9781003183976-5

autonomy and societal constraints. Those were the topics of the juvenile short stories (*On the Kitchen Steps*, *Virginity*), but also the main motifs of the prewar novel *Ferdydurke*. (As Włodzimierz Bolecki stresses, Gombrowicz had already conceptualized his notion of Form in the 1930s).[3] Form is the kind of identity that is only partially chosen or created by an individual; in most cases it is also given or implemented by the external forces on which one has, in most cases, very limited influence. The difficulty consists in the fact that there is no clear distinction between the external and the internal or between the biological and the cultural.[4] Form is not a piece of clothing that can be easily changed; rather, it has closer parallels to the human face. An individual can experiment and influence the look of their face in various ways (through skincare, make-up, face-covering headgear, facial hair styling, tattoos, piercing, or even through such advanced interventions as skin face transplants), but it is not possible to remove it like a mask.[5] And most crucially, the perception and final acknowledgment of one's face among other human beings is a result of constantly changing cultural and social norms, practices, and interactions,[6] as "[o]ne person creates the other," to use Gombrowicz's own summary of his philosophy of Form (PM 5). In the words of Bolecki, Form is "the universal product of social relations that deform human subjectivity."[7]

However, it is vital to point out that Gombrowicz's understanding of Form is primarily metaphysical and not political or sociological. In the remarks on *Ferdydurke* in his *Diary*, he notes that the questions of cultural, political, and social influence are of lesser importance for him than both the uncanny and fascinating act when concrete individualities mutually challenge and reshape their personalities.

> I do not deny that the individual is dependent on his milieu—but for me it is far more important, artistically far more creative, psychologically far more profound, and philosophically far more disturbing that man is also created by an individual man, by another person. In chance encounters. Every minute of the day. By virtue of the fact that I am always "for another," counting on someone else's seeing me, being able to exist in a specific manner only for someone else and by someone else, and existing—as a form—only through another.
> (D 288)

In Gombrowicz's eyes, the act of mutual creation is in most cases a result of an unusual or highly unexpected encounter of two (or more) individual and unique human beings. Such an encounter is in most cases an unpleasant experience, as it can quickly develop into a confrontation: intellectual, spiritual, or physical (see Chapter 2). But even in "normal" contact with other people one can observe mechanisms of the constant mutual influence and challenge. In one scene in *Ferdydurke*, the narrator Joey describes a conversation between Professor Pimko and Mrs. Youngblood, the mother of Zuta, the teenage schoolgirl. The argument centers around Zuta's impudent behavior, including her kicking Joey's leg. Pimko comments on the audacity of the young generation, while Mrs. Youngblood brushes off the incident as harmless and praises "the [modern] Era," a "great revolution in customs and traditions" (FER 114). When Pimko references Cyprian K. Norwid (1821–1883), a Polish Romantic poet, Zuta ostentatiously displays her ignorance, leading the professor to lament her nonchalance and disinterest in tradition. The scene highlights not only the generational gap and the changing values of society, but also the fact that the sheer presence of each of the four participants in the conversation—Joey, Pimko, Zuta, and Mrs. Youngblood—influences their behavior, reactions, and even the content of their utterances.

> The atmosphere became very pleasant indeed. The schoolgirl tossed her ignorance of Norwid to Pimko, Pimko tossed his shock at her ignorance of Norwid back to the schoolgirl, and the mother laughed within the Era. I alone sat there, excluded from the company, and I could not—I could not speak up, nor comprehend how the roles had been reversed, how this old relic, with legs a thousandfold worse than mine, was now in cahoots with the modern one against me, and how I had become a counterpoint to their melody.
>
> (FER 115–116)

Another common motif in Gombrowicz's prose is the irrational yet intense abomination and disgust that one can feel toward another person. In *Pornografia*, it is the feeling the main hero, Witold, experiences during a conversation with the officer of the Polish Home Army, Siemian.

> I didn't know what to do with him—and he couldn't help me because I had rejected him, thrown him out, and without him I found myself with regard to him—alone... as if I were holding him in my hand. And between me and him there was nothing but indifference, cold unfriendliness, revulsion, he was a stranger to me, he was disgusting!
>
> (POR 176)

In *Cosmos*, Gombrowicz's last novel, such an impenetrable revulsion toward a concrete person is presented from the opposite side: One of the novel's characters, Fuks, has a boss who cannot bear his physical presence for no explicable reason.

> We were undressing, and Fuks, shirt in hand, resumed his complaints about his boss, Drozdowski, he moaned whitely and wanly, carrot-like, that Drozdowski, that at first they got along famously, then something or other went sour, one way or another, I began to get on his nerves, can you imagine, I get on his nerves, let me move a finger and I get on his nerves, do you understand that, to get on your boss's nerves, seven hours a day, he can't stand me, he obviously tries not to look at me for seven hours straight, and

> if he happens to look at me his eyeballs skip away as if he'd been scalded, for seven hours! I don't know—Fuks went on, his eyes fixed on his shoes—sometimes I feel like falling on my knees and crying out: Forgive me, Mr. Drozdowski, forgive me! But forgive me for what? And it's not even his fault, I really do irritate him, my friends at work tell me shush, stay out of his sight, but—Fuks ogled me sadly, fish-like, with melancholy—but how can I keep in or out of his sight when we're together in the same room seven hours a day, if I clear my throat, move my hand, he breaks out in a rash.
>
> (COS 8–9)

Gombrowicz's conviction that a person's existence is reliant on being seen and recognized by someone else and that a human being is thus always interdependent with other people is particularly visible in his plays: *Princess Ivona* (1938), *The Marriage* (1948, 1953), and *Operetta* (1966).

The theater style of Gombrowicz is characterized by its embrace of absurdity, grotesque imagery, and black humor, all of which contribute to a provocative and unsettling theatrical experience that is to be situated within the broader tradition of the existentialism-inspired, European absurdist drama.[8] Gombrowicz's plays frequently use irrationality and absurdity to challenge traditional notions of "reality" and "identity," pushing the audience to confront the unpredictability of the world and the interhuman relationships. A prominent motif is dysfunctional family dynamics, with rebellious younger generations challenging the authority of their elders,[9] which explores the complexities of intersubjectivity, highlighting the tension between the individual self and external influences and structures that shape it. This is exemplified through examinations of different forms of living together, from the familial to the political, and the conflicts that arise from the clash of competing perspectives. Interestingly, Gombrowicz's dramatic works feature protagonists who are (or used to be, or want to be) kings, princes, princesses, and other members of the nobility, which on the one hand emphasizes the surreal and bizarre plot, but on the other hand alludes to the oeuvres of such representatives of classical European theater as William Shakespeare (1564–1616), Pedro Calderón de la Barca (1600–1681), Pierre Corneille (1606–1684), and Jean Racine (1639–1699).[10] In this context it is important to underline that neither Gombrowicz's *Princess Ivona* nor *The Marriage* could have been influenced by the canonical works of the Theater of the Absurd. To take two instances, Eugène Ionesco's *The Bald Soprano* was first performed in 1950, Samuel Beckett's *Waiting for Godot* in 1953.

That an individual can only exist through (and thanks to) the perception and influence of other people, is shown by Gombrowicz's very first play, ***Princess Ivona*** (also translated as ***Ivona, Princess of Burgundia***). Begun in 1933 and completed in 1935, the play was published in the journal *Skamander* in 1938. The first book edition (slightly modified) appeared twenty years later, in 1958. The play portrays Prince Philip, the next in line to the throne, encountering Ivona, a dull and unattractive girl, during a walk. Described by Gombrowicz as "awkward, apathetic, anaemic, shy, nervous and boring" (TES 49), Ivona initially repulses Philip. Yet, in an act of rebellion against social and aesthetic norms ("Why, pray, should only prettiness attract me. Who says so?," PLA 24), he proposes to her. This engagement, however, unleashes Ivona as a catalyst for the court's decay, as her many shortcomings expose the courtiers' own flaws and evils present and past.[11] Ivona's very presence, for instance, urges the king to recall a seamstress maid who committed suicide after being raped by him. Over time, each member of the court, including Philip himself, desires Ivona's demise, even though her only "fault" is being inept and anti-social, and thus tiring and annoying. She is eventually murdered in a wicked and grotesque way, by being served a bony pike during an official dinner. Ivona chokes on a fishbone and dies.

One can easily notice the intriguing parallel between *Princess Ivona* and existentialist literary masterpieces that explore the issue of intersubjectivity and being "for another," Albert Camus' novella *The Stranger* (1942) being a good example.[12] Both Ivona and Meursault, the main character of Camus' work, are portrayed as individuals who do not conform to societal norms or expectations, and who seem to be both unable and unwilling to connect with others on an emotional or interpersonal level. Meursault commits a homicide, but, as Camus suggestively presents, his punishment for this crime results mostly from the fact that the judge finds out that Mersault had not cried after his mother's death and showed no emotions during the burial. In other words, Meursault is not judged and convicted solely on the basis of murdering an Arab man, but also on the basis of how his other actions were perceived, remembered, and interpreted by other people. Ivona does not commit any crime, but the court's wish to kill her has similarly unfounded and irrelevant reasons, i.e., it is based exclusively on Ivona's social ineptitude and her inability to meet the expectations of the people surrounding her.

The death of Ivona brings relief to everyone at the court and restores the initial harmony between them. In the play's fourth act, Gombrowicz contrasts the horror of the absurd and cruel death of an innocent young woman with the power of the social rituals and the conviction that in such a situation "[o]ne must do something. One must say something" (PLA77), even if it means taking care of trifles or uttering platitudes.

Queen: *(nervous, perhaps slightly embarrassed)* Ignatius, we must start thinking about the court mourning. You haven't got a suitable suit. You have put on weight and they are all too small.

King: I haven't, have I? Well, I will order one.

Queen: Yes, but you must send for the tailor straight away.

King: (*surprised*) Tailor? Yes, of course… (*Rubs his eyes*) Yes, Solomon, the Tailor, men's outfitters. (*Looks at Ivona*). What? Dead. I mean—really dead.

Queen: *(after a moment)* We shall all die…

(PLA 77)

Figure 5.1 Alfred Camus (1945). Studio Harcourt. License: Public Domain.

In the closing scene, all the members of the court kneel in a final act of respect for the deceased Ivona, except for Prince Philip, who remains standing. The Chamberlain and the King chastise Philip for not kneeling, and the Queen tells him to follow suit ("All should be on their knees. And we all are," PLA 78). Eventually, Philip—who at the beginning of the play tried to rebel against hypocrisy and social norms—kneels down as well.

The question of intersubjectivity and the creation of the individual by another individual was taken to a new level in Gombrowicz's next play, ***The Marriage***. It was his first literary work composed in Argentina, written after he had completed the Spanish translation of *Ferdydurke* (see Chapter 3). The play was first published in Spanish under the title *El Casamiento* in Buenos

Aires in 1948. For the Polish edition, Gombrowicz had to wait five years: It was not until 1950 that he established contact with Jerzy Giedroyc, the founder and editor-in-chief of the leading Polish exile magazine *Kultura* and the publishing house Instytut Literacki (see Chapter 4). Subsequently, in 1953, *The Marriage* was published in book form, in one volume together with *Trans-Atlantyk*. Similarly to the masterpieces of the Theater of the Absurd, it is not easy to summarize the main plot of the play, as Gombrowicz follows in *The Marriage* the logic of a hallucination and the rapid and unexpected transformations of people and settings are thus to be taken for granted. Henry, a Polish soldier, has a dream (but is it really a dream? Or does human reality become nightmare-like?) in which his parents' house has been turned into a shabby pub: His father is an innkeeper, and his fiancée Molly is a maid and most probably a survivor of sexual violence. In the inn, the group of drunkards starts making trouble and harassing Henry's father. In an act of defense, the father proclaims himself to be untouchable "like a king" (PLA 113) and, consequently, he suddenly becomes a king. Henry thus becomes a prince and decides to marry Molly to "restore" her dignity. In the end, however, due to the suicide of Henry's friend, the marriage ceremony does not take place at all.

Despite its experimental form and unusual plot, *The Marriage* is a tribute to canonical European plays and shares many similarities with them. As Gombrowicz immodestly explained a few decades later, "*Hamlet* and *Faust* were my models, but only because of their quality of genius," TES 105). The reader can indeed recognize the allusions to *Hamlet*, *The Tempest*, *A Midsummer Night's Dream*, and *Macbeth* by William Shakespeare and *Life Is a Dream* by Pedro Calderón de la Barca, as well as to the Polish Romantic drama, for instance, the play *Balladyna* (1839) by Juliusz Słowacki.[13] Because of the main hero, who is clearly stylized as a "new" Hamlet—Hamlet in a modern, disenchanted and disillusioned world—*Marriage* is the most Shakesperean of Gombrowicz's plays.[14] In one of the culminative moments, Henry holds a longer monologue in which he denounces the lack a sense of a traditionally understood "self" and dismisses authorities, abstract concepts, and established beliefs. After renouncing faith in God and Reason, Henry expresses his desire to emerge in an interhuman connection with an authentic individual other than himself:

> [...] I'm not in need
> Of any attitude! I don't feel
> Other people's pain! I only recite
> My humanity! No, I do not exist.
> I haven't any 'I,' alas, I forge myself
> Outside myself, outside myself, alas, alas, oh the hollow
> Empty orchestra of my 'alas,' you rise up from my void
> And sink back into the void! [...]

I reject every order, every concept
I distrust every abstraction, every doctrine
I don't believe in God or in Reason!
Enough of these gods! Give me man!
May he be like me, troubled and immature,
confused and incomplete, dark and obscure,
so I can dance with him! Play with him! Fight with him!
Pretend to him! Ingratiate myself with him!
And rape him, love him and force myself
Anew from him, so I can grow through him, and in that way
Celebrate my marriage in the sacred human church!
(PLA 181–182)

The monologue delivered by Henry is also unique due to its sincere and unironic emotional intensity, which is a departure from Gombrowicz's usual distanced style.[15] As George Gömöri notices, through his assertion of the "sacred human church," on the one hand Gombrowicz attempts to resolve in *The Marriage* the tension between the individual and the collective, between the "I" and the "thou," and to position himself in support of the interconnectedness of humanity, but on the other hand he also highlights the inevitable Ferdydurkian "generalized inability" (*powszechna niemożność*) of such a project: "Henry's marriage [...] fails to take place (the Drunkards represent the disruptive force of instinct, similar to Ivona—hence the conceit of the Finger), and the revolution is a failure."[16] His sheer human condition makes Henry "a prisoner of Form" that cannot be overcome.[17]

Gombrowicz himself liked to associate the main ideas of *The Marriage* with the philosophy of Martin Buber (1878–1965), the Jewish religious philosopher and author of the canonical work *I and Thou* (1923) devoted to the philosophical aspects of interhuman relationships. At the time he was writing *The Marriage*, Gombrowicz read the recent Spanish translation of Buber's *The Problem of Man* (*Das Problem des Menschen*, 1942, 1948) and recognized in his interpretations of the classics of philosophy some themes that he found crucial for his own oeuvre.[18] Hoping to establish an intellectual acquaintance, and, no less importantly, to receive a few lines of endorsement that could help garner some interest in his play on the global book market, in 1951 Gombrowicz even sent a copy of the typescript to Buber in Israel. The language was not a barrier: Buber, then a professor at the University of Jerusalem, spoke fluent Polish, since in his youth he had attended a Polish high school (*gimnazjum*) in Lviv and before the war, some members of his family had belonged to the circles of engaged Polish intelligentsia in Galicia.[19] In his response to Gombrowicz, however, Buber showed no real interest in entering into long-lasting correspondence, even though he appreciated and praised the play, immediately recognizing its main topics: the tension between alienated individuals and the (im)possibility of authentic interactions between them.

Figure 5.2 Martin Buber (between 1940 and 1950). Author unknown. Public Domain.

In 1955, Buber finally wrote Gombrowicz a two-sentence endorsement note in French that ended with a short recommendation: "One should translate him" (*On devrait le traduire*).[20]

Within the Polish literary life of the time, the pivotal support for *The Marriage* and *Trans-Atlantyk* came from Józef Wittlin (1896–1976), an acknowledged Polish poet and writer of Jewish origin, then an émigré author living in New York. Wittlin wrote a preface to the first book edition (both works appeared in the same volume), in which he praised Gombrowicz's striving for truth and authenticity.[21] At the same time, Gombrowicz had begun to regularly publish in *Kultura* (see Chapter 4) from 1953 on, which also kindled curiosity in his literary work among Polish readers, both in the Polish People's Republic (where *Kultura* was smuggled in illegally) and abroad.[22] The rising interest in Gombrowicz's work was additionally boosted by the de-totaliatarianization of the Eastern and Central Europe, i.e. the death of Stalin (in 1953) and the changes throughout Eastern Block initiated by the "Secret Speech" held in February 1956 by the Soviet communist leader Nikita Khrushchev (1894–1971). Khrushchev admitted and condemned the crimes of Stalinism, thus opening a new chapter not only in Soviet domestic affairs but also on the international level, which was particularly noticeable in the countries that remained politically subordinated to the USSR. In the fall of 1956, in the Polish People's Republic there began a period of liberalization known as the "Polish October" or the "Polish Thaw," which brought about a relaxation of censorship and the re-appearance of the contemporary Western ("capitalist") artistic production in Polish cultural life: literature, philosophy, cinema, art, and theater. "Polish October" had a profound impact on Polish readers who were tired with years of compulsory Soviet-style socialist realism and thus very eager to embrace the audaciously rebellious style of Gombrowicz. In publicity materials on his works, Gombrowicz himself emphasized the significance of this moment, stating, "Finally! For ten years of the communist regime in Poland, it was forbidden to publish Gombrowicz or write about him. But now, since Gomółka [sic!] seized power, the regime has been mollified."[23] In accordance with the spirit of the "Polish Thaw," the communist authorities indeed allowed the publication of Gombrowicz's works (with the exception of *Diary*). Notably, the illustrations for the Polish postwar editions were created by leading avant-garde artists of the time, such as Daniel Mróz (1917–1993) for *Bacacay* (1957), Jan Młodożeniec (1929–2000) for *Trans-Atlantyk*, and *The Marriage* (1957) and Tadeusz Kantor (1915–1990) for *Princess Ivona* (1958).[24] Literary critics, particularly Artur Sandauer (1913–1989), helped to promote Gombrowicz's works and cement his status as a leading figure in Polish literature.

In words of David Brodsky, "Gombrowicz's spiritual presence" was widely felt among the Polish intelligentsia during the Thaw period,[25] as book publications came together with the first theater performances. In 1957, the play *Princess Ivona* was staged at the Teatr Dramatyczny in Warsaw, directed by the legendary actress and later anti-communist dissident Halina Mikołajska (1925–1989), and starring Barbara Krafft-Seidner (1928–2022) in the lead role. After half of a century, Krafft-Seidner (known in Poland as Barbara Krafftówna) described the experience of playing Ivona as "a leap into space" and noted that for her generation, the theater of Gombrowicz was "a departure from classical theater, from the form that had been established for generations. This literature changed the way we thought about theater. When we played Gombrowicz, we had the feeling of being in another world. [...] Many colleagues [...] treated his work almost like the Bible."[26] This sentiment was indeed shared by many of Krafft-Seidner's contemporaries.

Figure 5.3 Władysław Gomułka addresses hundreds of thousands of people in Warsaw on 24 October 1956. Author: Unknown. Public Domain. The "Polish October" was a political and social upheaval in Poland that led to significant political reforms.

In 1960, *The Marriage* had its world premiere in the Upper Silesian town of Gliwice, where it was directed by Jerzy Jarocki (1929–2012), one of the greatest representatives of Polish postwar theater. However, with the liberalization of the "Polish Thaw" on the wane, the production was halted by censors after just four performances, and *The Marriage* was not played again in Poland until the mid-1970s.[27]

Princess Ivona and *The Marriage* also marked a significant turning point in Gombrowicz's international recognition and popularity. Contrary to his prose works, which in most cases require readers some knowledge of the Polish and Argentinian contexts, his plays are kept on the level of abstraction that make them more universal. Of crucial significance was the French production of *The Marriage* directed by Jorge Lavelli (born in 1932). The play won first prize at the International Competition for Young Companies (*Concours des Jeunes Compagnies*) in June 1963 and was subsequently played at Théâtre Récamier in Paris from 1964. The play's success was not limited to the stage, as it also attracted significant interest from critics, marking the beginnings of Gombrowicz's international acknowledgment as a significant figure in contemporary theater and literature. Among the critics was the prominent Marxist philosopher and literary theorist Lucien Goldmann (1913–1970), who wrote an enthusiastic piece about the play itself. In his eyes, *The Marriage* is to be interpreted politically, through the lenses of Gombrowicz's aristocratic, Polish roots and identifying the turbulences of recent European history.[28] Such an oversimplifying and yet highly positive review written by the leading French intellectual must have been both flattering and embarrassing; Gombrowicz himself summarized his mixed feelings in his *Diary* in a half-provocative, half-resigned way:

> [Y]es, I do not deny that *The Marriage* is a wild version of a crazy history; in the dreamy or drunken becoming of this action is mirrored the fantasticality of the historical process, but to make Molly the nation and Father the state...?? Nothing doing. Goldmann, professor, critic, broad-shouldered Marxist, decreed that I did not know, that he knew better! Rabid Marxist imperialism! They use that doctrine to invade people! Goldmann, armed with Marxism, was the subject—I, deprived of Marxism, was the object [...].
>
> (D 670)[29]

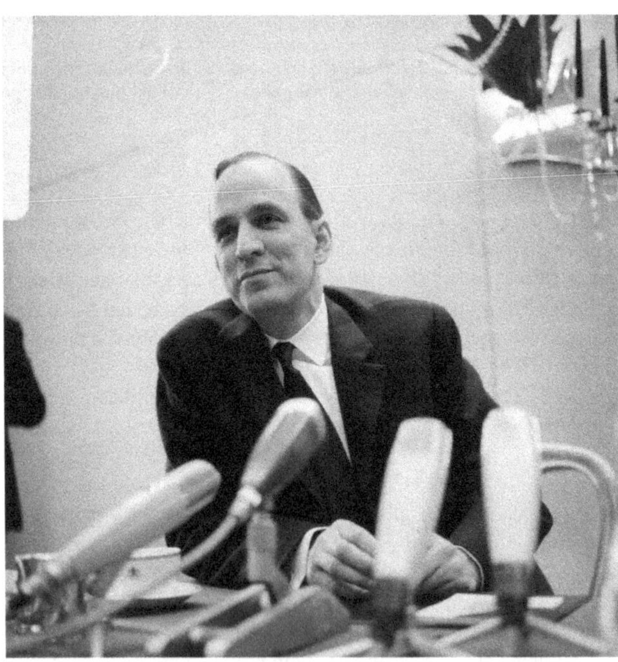

Figure 5.4 *Ingmar Bergman* (1966). Author: Joost Evers. Public Domain. In the 1960s, alongside his film work, Ingmar Bergman continued to be actively involved in theater productions.

The same year, Gombrowicz received a short but extraordinarily wholehearted letter from Ingmar Bergman (1918–2007), then the managing director of the prestigious Royal Dramatic Theatre (*Kungliga Dramatiska Teatern*) in Stockholm, who wrote "I want to tell you how happy I am for being in the position to perform your wonderful play *Yvonne* at my theatre! If possible[,] I will stage the play myself!"[30] *Princess Ivona* was indeed played in Stockholm in 1965, staged by one of the most prominent Swedish theater and film directors of the twentieth century, Alf Sjöberg (1903–1980); Bergman himself directed *Princess Ivona* a few decades later, in Munich in 1980 and Stockholm in 1995. Sjöberg's performance in the Royal Dramatic Theatre was an enormous success that also contributed to the international appreciation of Gombrowicz's work so that even the Nobel Prize in Literature was slowly becoming a realistic bet.

Gombrowicz's last theater play, ***Operetta*** (1966), introduces the motif of social revolution, presented in a grotesque and funny-strange manner, and at the same time again accentuates the significance of interhuman interactions in which the characters' desires and actions are molded by their perceptions of each other. At the heart of the story is the elegant Count Charmant, a dandy fashion enthusiast who devises a plan to seduce the young and inexperienced Albertine with the ultimate intention of transforming her through the act of "dressing up." However, his scheme takes an unexpected turn as Albertine's sexual desires are awakened, but she becomes fascinated not by Charmant's refined demeanor or stylish garments, but by the allure of complete nudity. Simultaneously, the renowned fashion dictator Fior (a reference to Christian Dior [1905–1957]),[31] is expected to visit Himalay Castle, which is the occasion to organize a grand costume ball. As the event reaches its peak, a gang of pickpockets ensures that chaos ensues, manners crumble, and costumes fall into disarray. Hufnagel, a horse lover and a rebel, takes charge and initiates a revolution. In the final act, the scene shifts to the ruins of the castle, where Hufnagel gallops after the representatives of the previous regime. Unexpectedly, Charmant enters, followed by a coffin which purportedly contains Albertine's lifeless body. Surprisingly, it is revealed that Albertine is alive, concealed within the coffin by the pickpockets. The play ends by hailing nudity and youth.

In the introductory commentary for the play, Gombrowicz admits that operetta as a literary form had always tempted him as a writer. "[The genre of] operetta, in its divine idiocy, in its heavenly sclerosis, in its glorious etherealness thanks to song, dance, gesture, and mask, seems to me the perfect theatre, perfectly theatrical" (PLA 203). The genre itself allows the use of repetition, gags, and some other elements of comicalness that are not always sophisticated (for instance, the Prince in *Operetta* "philosophically" observes that "there are faces which are inferior to arses," PLA 250). Gombrowicz's last play showcases his characteristic use of exaggeration and facetiousness that were absent in the toned down, reflective drama *The Marriage*, and thanks

Figure 5.5 *Kurt Jacobsson and Christian Dior* (1957). Author unknown. Public Domain. Christian Dior was a French designer whose "New Look" line, introduced in 1947, revolutionized fashion after the Second World War.

to its lighthearted cheerfulness, *Operetta* also significantly differs from the dark and grotesque humor of *Princess Ivona*. Although it introduces some more serious topics to play with (such as social inequalities, the decline of the feudal world, and revolutionary violence), it does it without caring much about ideological implications, the logic of the psychological development of the main characters, or even the consistency and reliability of the plot. In *Operetta*, the anarchic brilliance of Gombrowicz's humor goes in very different directions; the work satirizes among other things leftist public intellectuals who live in affluent capitalist societies by introducing the character of a Professor, a wretched and self-obsessed scholar who constantly vomits, clearly alluding to Jean-Paul Sartre and his most famous works: *Nausea* (1938), *Being and Nothingness* (1943), *Existentialism is Humanism* (1946), and essays *Situations* (1947–1976).[32]

Hufnagel: [...] *(kicks the PROFESSOR)* There!
Professor: Oh! God bless you! That is, bless you, but not God! There is no God. There is only a situation. I'm in a situation. I must choose. I choose revolution. I feel better now. The revolution!
Hufnagel: [...] I would remind you of Paragraph 137 B of our Revolutionary Theory.
Professor: 137B. Oh, yes, of course. According to that paragraph, my mentality is the mentality of a bourgeois, in other words, a mentality completely warped by class exploitation, so much so that everything I think and feel is perverted, sick, evil, false, erroneous... Consequently, my present anxiety is also warped, utterly corrupt at the root, and I should rid myself of it, expel it, dismiss it, disgorge it, eject it... Puuu.... Puuu.... Puke! Puke!
Hufnagel: A kick! *(he kicks him)*
Professor: Thanks! It's better now! Thanks! *(He wraps the seat of his pants)*
Oh, how I hate myself! [...]
I hate myself
But I likewise hate this hatred of mine
Because it's mine! A product of me!
Who is it that hates?
It is *I* who hate! I, a bourgeois!
I am the pathological product of a sick system
I, a morbid tumour, I, an ulcer, I, a disease
Consumed to the core by a social sin.
And so I hate myself... but I also hate
This hatred of mine... And again, I hate
The hatred of my hatred, which also hates
My hatred.... And I'm puking, puking, puking!
Hufnagel: You rotten scum...
(PLA 253–255)

Throughout the play, Albertine remains in a trance-like state, repeatedly whispering the word "nude" (*nagość*) with great yearning. The play ends with Charmant, Fior, and Firulet praising youth and nudity in a way that resemblances the final praise of the "eternal feminine" in Goethe's *Faust* ("O nudity, eternally youthful, hail!/O youth eternally nude, hail!," PLA 287). As George Gömöri notices, those words "convey [Gombrowicz's] biological optimism as well as his life-long insistence on unmasking, and on demolishing 'set' forms."[33] Nudity is thus seen not only as the opposite to the world of oversophisticated forms and norms represented by Charmant and Fior, but also as an attempt at phenomenological reduction and "bracketing" in the Husserlian sense: bracketing all cultural values, ideologies, schemes, and even Gombrowicz's own earlier concepts concerning the artificiality of human relationships.

Notes

1 See Husserl's *Cartesian Meditations*, particularly the last chapter: "Transcendental Being as Monadological Intersubjectivity" and §44 of that chapter: Edmund Husserl, *Cartesianische Meditationen: Eine Einleitung in die Phänomenologie*, ed. Elisabeth Ströker (Hamburg: Felix Meiner Verlag, 1995), 95–101.

2 Roman Ingarden, *Das literarische Kunstwerk: Eine Untersuchung aus dem Grenzgebiet der Ontologie, Logik und Literaturwissenschaft* (Halle (Saale): M. Niemeyer, 1931).

3 Włodzimierz Bolecki, "A Concise Companion to Polish Modernism," in *Being Poland: A New History of Polish Literature and Culture since 1918*, ed. Tamara Trojanowska et al., 105–131 (Toronto: University of Toronto Press, 2019), 127.

4 Olaf Kühl, "Ciało i jego maskowanie u Gombrowicza," *Teksty Drugie* 37, no. 1 (1996): 60.

5 Thus arises the question of authenticity, also one of the crucial motives of Gombrowicz's work: are we more authentic when we are naked or when wear clothing that we feel comfortable in and that help us to express ourselves? Cf. the opening of the article: George Gömöri, "The Antinomies of Gombrowicz," *The Modern Language Review* 73, no. 1 (1978): 119.

6 Cf. Błoński, *Forma, śmiech i rzeczy ostateczne*, 42.

7 Włodzimierz Bolecki, "A Concise Companion to Polish Modernism," in *Being Poland*, 127.

8 Thompson, *Witold Gombrowicz*, 44–43.

9 Jerzy Jarzębski, "Gombrowicz i Szekspir," *Pamiętnik Literacki* CV, no. 3 (2014): 82.

10 Ibid., 83.

11 Ibid.

12 Albert Camus, *The Stranger*, with the assistance of Matthew Ward (New York: Vintage International, 1989).

13 Jarzębski, "Gombrowicz i Szekspir,": 82; Bolecki, "Słowacki Gombrowicza,"; Suchanow, *Gombrowicz*, II 43, 49–51.

14 Jarzębski, "Gombrowicz i Szekspir,": 85.

15 The final part of this monologue was used as lyrics by the death metal band Behemoth in a song from their album *The Satanist*. The song featured the monologue spoken in Polish as a part of the track. Behemoth, "In the Absence Ov Light," in *The Satanist* (2014).

16 Louis Iribarne, "Revolution in the Theater of Witkacy and Gombrowicz," *The Polish Review* 18, no. 1/2 (1973): 73.

17 Ibid., 74.

18 Martin Buber, "Das Problem des Menschen," in *Schriften zu Philosophie und Religion*, ed. Ashraf Noor and Kerstin Schreck, 221–312, Martin Buber Werkausgabe Band 12 (Gütersloh: Gütersloher Verlagshaus, 2017). Cf. Suchanow, *Gombrowicz*, II 67–69.

19 Martin's uncle, Rafał Buber (1866–1931), was an esteemed Galician attorney and a member of the Polish Socialist Party, as well as a deep friend of one of the most significant Polish Marxist philosophers, Stanisław Brzozowski (1878–1911). Martin Buber also advised on the first attempts at translations of Brzozowski's works into German. Aleksandra Konarzewska, "Immer ist etwas da, das dem Menschen den

Menschen stiehlt.": Stanisław Brzozowski – Marxismus als Philosophie der Kultur und Entfremdung," in *Der Geschichtsmaterialismus als Kulturphilosophie und andere Schriften*, ed. Aleksandra Konarzewska and Alexander K. Golec, 9–32 (Stuttgart: Ibidem Verlag, 2021), 13.

20 This happened as in 1955 Gombrowicz attempted anew to establish some contacts with Buber, this time through the Polish-Jewish writer Leo Lipski (1917–1997), who was then living in Israel. Martin Buber and Witold Gombrowicz, "Korespondencja między Witoldem Gombrowiczem a Martinem Buberem," in *Gombrowicz w Argentynie: Świadectwa i dokumenty 1939–1963*, ed. Rita Gombrowicz, 162–169 (Kraków: Wydawnictwo Literackie, 2004); Martin Buber, [Letter], July 9, 1951, GEN MSS 515 Box 2 f. 52, Witold Gombrowicz Archive, Beinecke Rare Book and Manuscript Library, Yale University; Piotr Sadzik, "Listy Witolda Gombrowicza do Leo Lipskiego," *Teksty Drugie*, no. 6 (2020).

21 The idea to publish both works together came from Jerzy Giedroyc. Józef Wittlin, "Uwagi wstępne," in *Trans-Atlantyk. Ślub: (Z wstępem Józefa Wittlina i komentarzem autora)*, 7–21 (Paryż: Instytut Literacki, 1953).

22 Jerzy Giedroyc, "[Wspomnienie, 29.07.1984]," in *Gombrowicz w Europie: Świadectwa i dokumenty 1963–1969*, ed. Rita Gombrowicz, 48–50 (Kraków: Wydawnictwo Literackie, 2002).

23 My translation. Witold Gombrowicz, *Jak czytają Gombrowicza w kraju ("Ferdydurke" i "Dziennik"); Krótka historia "Ferdydurke"* [Publicity material in Polish, typescript carbon, typescript annotated (photocopy)/n.d.], GEN MSS 515 Box 12 f. 448, Witold Gombrowicz Archive, Beinecke Rare Book and Manuscript Library, Yale University.

24 David Brodsky, "Witold Gombrowicz and the "Polish October"," *Slavic Review* 39, no. 3 (1980): 464.

25 Ibid., 467.

26 "Czasami skakałam w kosmos: [Interview with Barbara Krafft-Seidner]," *Rzeczpospolita* (02.12.2008), https://www.rp.pl/teatr/art7925741-czasami-skakalam-w-kosmos (accessed May 18, 2021).

27 Jacek Kopciński, "Drama as a Manifold Portrait: Polish Drama After the Second World War," in *Being Poland: A New History of Polish Literature and Culture since 1918*, ed. Tamara Trojanowska et al., 535–569 (Toronto: University of Toronto Press, 2019), 540–545. Despite the challenges posed by censorship after the end of the "Polish Thaw," Gombrowicz's plays continued to be performed on stage in communist Poland, and in fact, during the 1970s and 1980s it was often easier for people to become familiar with his works through theater productions than through books, as the 1957 and 1958 editions were quickly sold out. Filipowicz, "Fission and Fusion,": 163–164.

28 Goldmann later wrote a paper in which he interpreted *Princess Ivona* and *The Marriage* through Gombrowicz's gentry roots and—because of his Polishness—his assumed Catholicism, without caring much about the fact that the literary world of Gombrowicz had been always consequently atheist and his attitude toward the gentry as a social class remained ambivalent at best. Lucien Goldmann, "The Theatre of Gombrowicz," *The Drama Review: TDR* 14, no. 3 (1970). In the same text, Goldmann wanted to see in *The Marriage* an allusion to the Stalin–Trotsky conflict. Goldmann, "The Theatre of Gombrowicz,": 110.

29 In *France Observateur*, Gombrowicz published in 1964 the short text *What Is the Sense of "The Marriage"* (*Quel est le sens du «Mariage»*), in which he thanked Goldmann and appreciated his review, yet also politely indicated some more philosophical ways of reading this play. Witold Gombrowicz, "Jaki jest sens "Ślubu," in *Polemiki i dyskusje*, ed. Włodzimierz Bolecki, 137–139, Varia 2 (Kraków: Wydawnictwo Literackie, 2004).

30 The letter was written in English. Ingmar Bergman, [*Letter*], November 2, 1964, GEN MSS 515 Box 1 f. 28, Witold Gombrowicz Archive, Beinecke Rare Book and Manuscript Library, Yale University.

31 In the initial versions of the *Operetta*, his name was Dior. See the typescript of *Operetta* with Gombrowicz's pen corrections, where "Dior" was replaced everywhere with "Fior": Witold Gombrowicz, *Operetka* [IV] [typescript, carbon, corrected], 1966, GEN MSS 515 Box 15 f. 534, Witold Gombrowicz Archive, Beinecke Rare Book and Manuscript Library, Yale University.

32 On role of Sartre for Gombrowicz's work, see: Renato Barilli, "Sartre i Camus w *Dzienniku*," in *Gombrowicz filozof*, ed. Francesco M. Cataluccio and Jerzy Illg, 227–239 (Kraków: Społeczny Instytut Wydawniczy Znak, 1991), 232. Cf. Miłosz, *Rok myśliwego*, 281.

33 Gömöri, "The Antinomies of Gombrowicz,": 127.

6 Being and Nothingness

It is often emphasized that among Gombrowicz's works, his prose and drama plays are much "more philosophical" than some attempts at purely philosophical writing (such as an essay on existentialism, or a posthumously published collection of lectures, *A Guide to Philosophy in Six Hours and Fifteen Minutes*).[1] Indeed, while reading *Ferdydurke*, *Trans-Atlantyk*, or *Diary*, one finds it hard to escape the thought that author's metaphysical reflections result not from tedious studies of treatises that concern the question why there is something rather than nothing, but from intelligence, talent for observation, and readiness to discuss abstract ontological questions (such as substance, causation, existence, unity, or plurality), but on his own terms, in a relaxed and non-scholarly way.

A good example of this is the novel *Ferdydurke*, where a significant role is played by the ontological dialectic between the whole and the parts, reflecting the disintegration of reality and the dissolution of social norms and structures and corresponding to the fragmented human self-perception and self-assertion. This is shown particularly well by the chapter "The Child Runs Deep in Filidor" (FER 87–101),[2] where the all-encompassing disintegration is illustrated with the examination of the body as individual parts (to take one instance, "calves" in the Ferdydurkian universe stand for modernity, progress, and youth). Furthermore, *Ferdydurke* explores such themes as the disintegration of language and literature into mere words, slogans, and platitudes, which becomes additionally accelerated by the growing significance of mass media and popular culture (cf. Chapter 4). This dialectic of decomposition allows the emergence of new forms; however, these new compositions often lack coherence and fail to correspond harmoniously with one another, revealing the tensions inherent to the process of disintegration and reformation. In *Ferdydurke*, as well as in other prewar works by Gombrowicz (see Chapter 5), one can also notice philosophical themes characteristic of existentialist philosophy, such as boredom and the absurdity of existence.[3] As Michał P. Markowski notices, in Gombrowiczian realm, boredom, stupidity, and absurdity are closely related[4]; boredom even guarantees a certain "facticity of existence."[5] In this context it suffices to mention the famous scene of

DOI: 10.4324/9781003183976-6

the lesson on Polish literature in *Ferdydurke*, in which students are bored to tears with the school ceremonial of brainless veneration of "great poets," so that when the teacher starts the ritual of explaining the greatness of the poet Juliusz Słowacki ("I'll recite for you my lesson, and then in your turn you'll recite yours," FER 41–41), they react with behavior typical of weary students: carving on desktops with pocket knives and throwing small paper balls into the inkwells. In Gombrowicz's later works, the general tone becomes gradually darker and more sinister while introducing further ontological motifs. In *Trans-Atlantyk*, one of the major themes is an all-encompassing emptiness and silence,[6] whereas in *Pornografia*, the question of youth and beauty is confronted with the transience of human existence and one's own physical decay (see Chapter 3).

The quieter, yet more ominous atmosphere of Gombrowicz's later works contrasts with the fact that the last years of the 1950s and the early 1960s marked an important turning point in his literary career. Parallel to its re-emergence on the cultural market in Poland (see Chapter 5), Gombrowicz's oeuvre was "discovered" by Konstanty A. Jeleński (1922–1987), a brilliant Polish émigré essayist and intellectual, and by François Bondy (1915–2003), the Swiss journalist, translator, author, and the founder of the French magazine *Preuves*. Both Jeleński and Bondy were well-connected in intellectual and cultural life in postwar Europe, and thanks to their authentic, passionate engagement in endorsing the experimental and "exotic" prose of the unknown writer from Buenos Aires it could slowly appear on the European book market. The French edition of *Ferdydurke* was published in 1958, the German in 1960; in 1961, there appeared the English translation of *Ferdydurke*, the French edition of *Pornografia*, and the German edition of *Diary*. Crowning proof for the rising gravity of Gombrowicz as an internationally acknowledged author was his receiving a well-paid residence in West Berlin from the Ford Foundation in 1963. This meant moving back to Europe, after almost a quarter of a century of living in Buenos Aires, yet Gombrowicz did not hesitate to accept the American invitation. As a guest of the Foundation, he spent a whole year (1963–1964) in West Berlin, shortly after the Berlin Wall had been erected. He could thus witness not only the most symbolical and obvious exemplification of the Cold War division of Europe but also the final years of the postwar latency in German society, as the crucial years of the leftist revolt, as well as Willy Brandt's turn to *Ostpolitik*, were still to come.[7]

Unfortunately, the stay in Berlin was disturbed by a series of both minor and major misfortunes, first and foremost various health issues that required longer hospitalizations. Gombrowicz's Argentinian way of life, which consisted of spending long hours in cafes and participating in jocund and absurd discussions, was no longer possible due to the cultural differences and a language barrier: he did not speak German, and his potential partners spoke neither French nor Spanish. (However, at the same time he remained very active sexually; in

Figure 6.1 *East Berlin near Bernauer Strasse* (1961). Author: The Central Intelligence Agency. Public Domain. The construction of the Berlin Wall in 1961 physically divided East and West Berlin, symbolizing the broader Cold War divide.

June 1963 he wrote in a letter to Jeleński: "a terrible attack of pederasty [sic!] got me; I don't do anything else but that [sex], with so far four young German men [*z Niemczykami*], God forbid, at my age!").[8] Finally, contact with the Central European nature in Berlin parks brought the recollection of his youth in rural Poland, leading to the realization of his own age and transience. In *Diary*, one can find the following passage on the walk in the park in Tiergarten:

> It was then (while walking in the Tiergarten) that I caught a certain scent, a mixture of herbs, water, stone, wood bark, I couldn't say what exactly… yes, Poland, this was Polish, just like in Małoszyce, Bodzechów, my childhood, yes, yes, the same, why, it wasn't too far away now, a stone's throw away, the same nature… which I had left behind a quarter of a century earlier. Death. The cycle was coming to a close. I had returned to those scents, therefore, death. Death. […] I should not have left America.
>
> (D 626)

Yet perhaps the most devastating experience was the orchestrated, malicious political provocation by the Polish security service (*Służba Bezpieczeństwa*, SB), which involved sending their secret agent, Barbara Witek-Swinarska, to

Berlin. Privately known as the wife of the renowned Polish-German theater director Konrad Swinarski, Witek-Swinarska asked Gombrowicz to meet in a Berlin café, to which Gombrowicz agreed. Shortly thereafter, she published an article in a Polish magazine that manipulatively distorted some of Gombrowicz's statements, falsely portraying him as a defender of Nazis and someone who made derogatory remarks about the victims of Nazi rule in Poland. This issue struck a sensitive chord for Poles at the time,[9] particularly due to the German Federal Republic's ongoing reluctance to confront its recent past. (The first major trials of Nazi perpetrators conducted by the German state apparatus, the *Frankfurter Auschwitzprozesse*, did not begin until December 1963; additionally, the postwar border with Poland was still not officially recognized by West Germany.)[10] In this context, Witek-Swinarska craftily and deviously exploited Gombrowicz's fame as a "critic of Polishness" (see Chapter 4) by attributing statements to him such as "Poles are parochial nationalists by birth and by conviction. […] And that Polish tendency to exaggerate. It is only in your country where one discusses the horrors that happened during the war. […] Distance. Distance. This is what you lack."[11] Witek-Swinarska's text also addressed Gombrowicz's decision to remain in Argentina during the Second World War and the fact that he happened to meet some Germans there (she attributed to Gombrowicz the statement "I have great respect for Germans as a nation"[12]), slyly alluding to the fact that after the war many high-ranking Nazis, including Adolf Eichmann and Josef Mengele, had found safe haven under Juan Perón's rule.

The intrigue coordinated by the *Służba Bezpieczeństwa* proved successful, as Witek-Swinarska's manipulative text provoked a tremendous outcry in the Polish press, both within the Polish People's Republic and abroad. Initially, Gombrowicz was naïvely convinced that Witek-Swinarska was yet another person who could have simply misunderstood him, so he attempted to clarify the situation by sending corrections to Polish newspapers and cultural institutions. However, only the circle around Giedroyc's *Kultura* was willing to listen to him and took his side,[13] immediately recognizing Witek-Swinarska's publication as part of the broader anti-Western campaign by the Polish communist regime.[14] Deeply hurt by the fact that leading Polish and Polish-Jewish writers and authors were uninterested in hearing his version of the encounter with Witek-Swinarska and instead publicly attacked him,[15] Gombrowicz made the decision not to even visit his native country.[16] Instead, after the Ford scholarship expired, he moved to France, where during a conference in Abbaye de Royaumont he met Marie-Rita Labrosse (b. 1935), a Canadian literary scholar, who became his partner and future wife. In the fall of 1964, they both settled in Vence (a small town in Provence, close to Nice), where they lived together to the end of Gombrowicz's life.

In Vence, Gombrowicz finished his last novel, which he began writing in Argentina and on which he worked in Berlin. ***Cosmos*** (*Kosmos*, 1965), again, is a first-person narrative told by a certain Witold, who spends his holiday in a bed and breakfast in Zakopane, a small, yet much-frequented Carpathian town at the foot of the Tatra Mountains in southern Poland. Whereas the plots of Gombrowicz's previous novels are difficult to summarize because of their absurdity or illogicality, *Cosmos* in fact does not have a typical plot at all—the reader follows the stream of consciousness of the main protagonist, who has a feeling that the reality surrounding him is somehow at stake[17] and thus tries to discover meaning in everything he experiences: objects, events, gestures, and other people. Through Witold's mind, *Cosmos* offers an attempt to synthesize reality through (unsuccessful) seeking how to turn the meaningless into the meaningful.[18] But despite his efforts, the disturbingly coincidental and contingent chain of things, events, and experiences does not reveal any logic or sense (not to mention causal relations)[19]; in the best case, one can only realize the callous mechanisms of the unruffled temporal order—and that leads to the realization that one's own existence is transient and finite.

Figure 6.2 Rock Refuge of Reverend Stolarczyk in the Tatra Mountains (1876). Author: Walery Eljasz-Radzikowski. Public Domain. Before the Second World War, Tatra Mountains and Zakopane were popular destinations among Polish elites and intellectuals.

This metaphysical discovery, however, is eventually verbalized not by Witold, but by Leon, a middle-aged former bank manager. At the beginning of the novel, Leon is depicted as a quintessential conservative, middle-aged family man, characterized by limited intellectual horizons, a peculiar sense of humor, and a penchant for jokes and wordplay that elicit laughter mostly from himself. His way of speaking is filled with nonsensical neologisms, diminutives, and phrases such as "Ti-ri-ri! Grażyna mine [...], why don't you toss your Daddydaddy some radishy foodie food? Toss it!" (COS 21). However, as Konstanty Jeleński notices, Leon is in fact Witold's doppelgänger, the only one who is able to sense "cracks of existence" (to use Jolanta Brach-Czaina's term) in the most trivial aspects of daily life; "a sort of genius," in the words of Jeleński, "who understands everything, and above all the stupidity of banality."[20] It is Leon who in a conversation with Witold dares to describe the essence of transience and nothingness—yet in his own very special style:

> "What's so amusing?"
>
> "What? Nothing! Exactly that: nothing! Ha, that's a language game, if you please, hm… I'm amused by 'nothing,' mark you, Your Reverence, my venerable companion and merry-maker and horse-drawn carriage, because 'nothing' is exactly what we do all our lives. A fellow stands, sits, talks, writes and… nothing. A fellow buys, sells, marries, doesn't marry and—nothing. A fellow sitzum on a stumpium and—nothing. Soda pop."
>
> [...]
>
> He pondered and blew on his hands.
>
> "It's run through my fingers!"
>
> "What has?"
>
> He replied nasally, monotonously: "Years disintegrate into months, months into days, days into hours, minutes into seconds, seconds run past. You won't catch them. Everything runs past. Flies away. Who am I? I am a certain number of seconds—that have run past. The result: nothing. Nothing."
>
> He flared up and exclaimed: "It's thievery!"
>
> (COS 130–131)

Leon's particular manner of speaking reveals a further feature of *Cosmos*, namely that the uncertainty of language is meant to reflect the uncertainty of the world.[21] This emphasizes, for instance, the recurrence of the prewar slogan *swój do swego po swoje* throughout the novel. As the translator Danuta Borchardt explains, "[l]iterally it means 'himself to his own for his own,' and it refers to buying stuff from your own people—a distant cousin to 'buy American,' or, more personally, 'getting one's gratification from one's own.'"[22]

In the twentieth century, it should be added, this slogan had a double dimension: before the First World War, it was an expression of solidarity against and resistance to the German policies that systemically discriminated against Poles in various fields, including trade. In the interwar period, on the other hand, it was appropriated by Polish nationalists to exhort the public boycott of Jewish merchants. In *Cosmos*, however, this slogan (as well as a Polish saying, "scraping a turnip just for yourself," COS 137)[23] is ridiculed through usage in onanistic-solipsist contexts (the triple usage of the word *swój*, "one's own," indeed invites some unsophisticated wordplay),[24] and thus it is depoliticized in a typically Gombrowiczian, absurd way.

Finally, *Cosmos* again questions the sharp distinction between the human and the natural.[25] Witold's determined hunt for meaning in a disenchanted, absurd world involves absurd, senseless killing a cat and foolish play with its dead body. The death of a cat, together with the previous death of a sparrow, announces a metaphysical horror, ultimately proven with the later death of Ludwik.

> I was reaching the porch. Lena's cat, Davie, sat on the banister and, on seeing me, it stood up and stretched itself so that I would tickle it. I caught the cat tightly by the throat, I began to strangle it—what am I doing—flashed through me like lightning, but then I thought: too bad, it's too late, I tightened my fingers with all my might. I strangled it. It hung limp.
>
> What now, what next, I was on the porch with a strangled cat in my hands, something had to be done with the cat, lay it down somewhere, hide it? [...] I deliberated, the cat weighed heavily on me, I couldn't make up my mind, all was quiet, but suddenly my eye fastened on a tough string that tied a small tree to its pole, one of those trees white with lime, I untied the string, made a loop, I looked around wondering if anyone could see me (the house was asleep, no one would have believed that not so long ago a din had swept through here), I remembered there was a hook in the wall, I don't know what for, perhaps for hanging laundry, I carried the cat there, it wasn't far, about twenty paces from the porch, I hung it on the hook. It hung like the sparrow, like the stick, completing the picture.
>
> (COS 70–71)

Paralleling the metaphysical inquiries with attention to the question of animals—their silent, yet pervasive presence in the world—becomes less surprising when one considers that the philosophers who truly and genuinely inspired Gombrowicz were those who considered animals as a source of philosophical reflection and intellectual challenge. "When I play with my cat, how do I know that she is not playing with me rather than I with her?," was the rhetorical question posed by Michel de Montaigne (1533–1592), one of Gombrowicz's favorite authors.[26] The famous encounter with a cow described in *Diary* can be seen as a subtle tribute to Friedrich Nietzsche's essay *On the Use and Abuse of History for Life* (1874), where in the opening passages the author contemplates a grazing herd and highlights their remarkable ability to exist solely in the present moment, devoid of any preoccupation with the past or the future.[27] Nietzsche argues that while humans aspire to emulate the carefree existence of animals, they are hindered by their inability to possess the same willful abandonment, because they grapple with the weight of the past, perpetually clinging to memories that disrupt their tranquility. Gombrowicz, on the other hand, describes in *Diary* his feeling of intellectual discomfort (both epistemological and ontological) while being confronted face-to-face with the other animal species:

> I was walking along a eucalyptus-lined avenue when a cow sauntered out from behind a tree.
>
> I stopped and we looked each other in the eye.
>
> Her cowness shocked my humanness to such a degree—the moment our eyes met was so tense—I stopped dead in my tracks and lost my bearings *as a man*, that is, as a member of the human species. The strange feeling that I was apparently discovering for the first time was the shame of a man come face-to-face with an animal. I allowed her to look and see me—this made us equal—and resulted in my also becoming an animal—but a strange even forbidden one, I would say.
>
> [...]
>
> Cows.
>
> When I pass a herd of cows, they turn their heads toward me and their eyes do not leave me until I pass. Just like at the Russoviches' in Corrientes. But then I paid no attention, whereas now, after the matter of "the cow who saw me," these looks seem like seeing to me. Grass and herbs! Trees and fields! The green nature of the world! I immerse myself in this expanse as if I were pushing off from shore and a presence consisting of a billion beings overwhelms me.
>
> (D 307–308, Gombrowicz's emphasis)

As Paweł Mościcki observes, for Gombrowicz, the differentiation between humans and animals is a process that allows humans to shape their sense of self. Simultaneously, it makes it impossible to comprehend animals in their own essence without reference to one's own humanness.[28] The ruminations on animals in the *Diary* thus conclude with the question, "The cow. How am I supposed to act toward a cow?," which quickly becomes generalized to encompass nature as a whole, leading to the query, "Nature. How am I supposed to behave toward nature?" (D 309).[29]

The most significant parallels in the contemplation of human and nonhuman subjects can be found between Gombrowicz and the German philosopher Arthur Schopenhauer (1788–1860). The influence of Schopenhauer's work is noticeable in many of Gombrowicz's writings,[30] but the similarities are particularly striking in the second and third volumes of the *Diary*. In these volumes, Gombrowicz gradually moves away from transient political debates and literary trends, turning his ruminations toward the sphere of practical philosophy. He does it in his characteristically implicit manner, through observations and descriptions of his immediate surroundings and without explicit references or name-dropping, yet the presence of Schopenhauerian motifs is indisputable. Schopenhauer is one of the first Western philosophers to reject the primacy of reason as the guarantee for the metaphysical superiority of humans (which echoes in Gombrowicz's conviction that "the imperialism of reason is horrible," D 228). Instead, he focuses on the similarities rather than differences between humans and animals, emphasizing that animals possess certain determining characteristics that warrant their consideration as subjects of moral philosophy, namely, some instinctual dispositions and the capacity for suffering. From this follows Schopenhauer's conviction that the crucial notion for ethics should not be "happiness" (as Aristotle wanted) or "dignity" (as Kant wanted), but "compassion" (German: *Mitleid*), particularly compassion toward those beings who are able to feel suffering. In his influential 1840 work on ethics, Schopenhauer argues against excessively complicated moral systems[31] and argues that compassion is the only truly moral motivation, inseparably intertwined with the animal question. He asserts that "compassion for animals is so closely associated with goodness of character that one may confidently assert that whoever is cruel to animals could not be a good person."[32] For Schopenhauer, cruelty, rather than dishonesty (as Kant attempted to demonstrate), represents the gravest moral evil. As he passionately argues, "[n]othing so shakes the deepest ground of our moral feeling as cruelty. We can pardon any other crime, only not cruelty."[33]

According to Maja Kittel, it is precisely in the conviction that genuine philosophy has its roots in sensitivity toward suffering that perhaps the most significant affinity between Gombrowicz and Schopenhauer lies.[34] Within *Diary*, one finds various contemplations Schopenhauerian in spirit on the broader acceptance of exploiting, tormenting, and killing animals by humanity (cf. Chapter 2), sometimes discretely veiled by irony and provokingly naïve assertions, e.g. while intentionally criticizing horseback riding as a leisure activity in a discussion with his friends in Argentina ("A man on a horse is as weird as a rat riding a rooster, a chicken riding a camel, a monkey riding a cow, or a dog riding a buffalo. A man on a horse is a scandal, an upsetting of the natural order of things, violent artificiality, dissonance, ugliness," D 307). Such remarks are intertwined with much more serious ruminations on cruelty and the nature of pain, which finally leads to a conclusion that the question of physical pain requires overcoming the traditional, reason-based distinction between an animal and a human.[35] Compassion, as Włodzimierz Bolecki notices, is present

Figure 6.3 *Arthur Schopenhauer* (1859). Author: Johann Schäfer. Public Domain. Schopenhauer was a German philosopher who emphasized the importance of compassion and pity toward all sentient beings.

in Gombrowicz's literary works only in contexts of animals', not humans' deaths.[36] For Gombrowicz, the anthropocentrism of Western culture—Christianity (exemplified in *Diary* by the Roman Catholicism),[37] Marxism,[38] but also the dominant currents in literature and philosophy of the twentieth century (existentialism)—prevented it from noticing that the question of physical pain should be conceived to be a crucial question concerning the existence of any living being, i.e. a question that philosophically challenges the traditionally understood notion of being and nothingness.

> No matter what we are told, there exists, in the entire expanse of the Universe, throughout the whole space of Being, one and only one awful,

> impossible, unacceptable element, one and only one thing that is truly and absolutely against us and absolutely devastating: pain. It is on pain and on nothing else that the entire dynamic of existence depends. Remove pain and the world becomes a matter of complete indifference…
>
> What am I saying! Perhaps this is too serious a subject for mere philosophical discourse… Truly menacing! I would like to note that for those thinkers [contemporary French philosophers] the world is always, in spite of everything, a place for rather calm, if not Olympian, cerebral speculation. All of these analyses are healthy inasmuch as they are produced by professors who are pretty well off and rather comfortably seated in their armchairs. The completely childlike ignorance of pain is at the base of this tireless playing with intellectual blocks.
>
> (D 699)

Thus it should come as no surprise that in his late essays (posthumously included in the second edition of the third volume of *Diary*), devoted to Dante's *Divine Comedy* and fueled with a fresh reading of Michel Foucault's (1926–1984) and Ronald Barthes' (1915–1980) philosophical writings, Gombrowicz repeats his conviction: there is an abyss between the sphere of the rational and the physical, and the issue of physical pain and simple compassion toward those who suffer is much more important than any theory, system, or literary masterpiece. How could Dante maintain the perspective of a pious Catholic while watching the torments of the Inferno? Why did he not question the concept of a punishment that no longer has an aim (neither purification nor compensation nor reconciliation) but is merely revenge? Why the perspective of a bored tourist who reports on eternal suffering in such an unruffled way?

Following his move to France in 1964, the hardships and existential uncertainties of the past gave way to a more stable period for Gombrowicz. Besides the successes of the plays *The Marriage* and *Princess Ivona* (see Chapter 5), in 1967 *Cosmos* received the prestigious International Prix Formentor Prize, renowned at the time as an accolade comparable to the Nobel Prize (previous recipients included Jorge Luis Borges and Saul Bellow). However, Gombrowicz's health steadily declined, and according to the recollections of Jan Błoński, he harbored bitterness toward his body's ongoing "betrayal" and the belated arrival of certain stabilizing elements in his life.[39] Amidst the tumultuous events of 1968, Gombrowicz displayed little genuine interest in the transformative developments reshaping postwar Europe, be it in Czechoslovakia, Poland, or France. Two months after conducting a series of private mini-lectures on philosophy for his wife Rita and the French writer and literary critic Dominique de Roux (1935–1977), Gombrowicz passed away in 1969 in Vence, where his final resting place can be found.

Notes

1 Janusz Margański, "Filozof Gombrowicz," *Teksty Drugie* 11, no. 5 (1991): 112.
2 Cf. Janusz Margański, "Między powiastką a filozofią: O 'Ferdydurke' Witolda Gombrowicza," *Pamiętnik Literacki*, no. 1 (2000): 134–136.
3 Francesco M. Cataluccio, "Gombrowicz filozof," in *Gombrowicz filozof*, ed. Francesco M. Cataluccio and Jerzy Illg, 5–24 (Kraków: Społeczny Instytut Wydawniczy Znak, 1991), 12.
4 Michał P. Markowski, "'Indomitable Boredom Above the Entire World': Gombrowicz (and Other Polish Writers) on Existential Predicament," in *Gombrowicz in Transnational Context: Translation, Affect, and Politics*, ed. Silvia G. Dapía, 97–114 (New York: Routledge, 2019), 105–107.
5 Ibid., 101–103.
6 Jaroslaw Anders, *Between Fire and Sleep: Essays on Modern Polish Literature* (New Haven, Ann Arbor, Michigan: Yale University Press, 2009), 40; George Gasyna, "Toward Heterotopia: The Case of "Trans-Atlantyk," *Slavic Review* 68, no. 4 (2009): 902; Bhambry, Tul'si (Tuesday), "'The Quieter the Louder Indeed,'" in *Gombrowicz in Transnational Context.*
7 Andrzej S. Kowalczyk, "'Their Astounding Strength in Overcoming Their Past…': The Memory of Nazism in the Berlin Diary," in *Gombrowicz in Transnational Context: Translation, Affect, and Politics*, ed. Silvia G. Dapía, 208–224 (New York: Routledge, 2019), 219–221.
8 My translation. Witold Gombrowicz, "[Letter, 15.VI.1963]," in *Gombrowicz: Walka o sławę*, ed. Jerzy Jarzębski, 97–98 2 (Kraków: Wydawnictwo Literackie, 1998), 97.
9 Andrzej S. Kowalczyk, "'Their Astounding Strength in Overcoming Their Past…,'" in *Gombrowicz in Transnational Context*, 218.
10 An insight into how the Polish intelligentsia of the time conceived of that issue is provided by the short and bitter poem "Innocence" by Wisława Szymborska (1923–2012) from the volume *No End of Fun* (1967): "Conceived on a mattress made of human hair/Gerda. Erika. Maybe Margarete./She doesn't know, no, not a thing about it. (…) The company she works for plans to export/the finest mattresses, synthetic fiber only./Trade brings nations closer." Wisława Szymborska, *Nic dwa razy/Nothing Twice: Wybór wierszy/Selected Poems*, with the assistance of Stanisław Barańczak, and Clare Cavanagh (Kraków: Wydawnictwo Literackie, 2012), 93.
11 My translation. Barbara Witek-Swinarska, "O dystansie, czyli rozmowa z mistrzem," in *Polemiki i dyskusje*, ed. Włodzimierz Bolecki, 153–160, Varia 2 (Kraków: Wydawnictwo Literackie, 2004), 158.
12 Ibid., 157.
13 See the articles by Konstany Jeleński and Ludwik Mieroszewski, published in *Kultura* no. 10 and 12 (1963). Konstanty A. Jeleński, "Pokajanie Picassa i zdrada Gombrowicza," in *Polemiki i dyskusje*, ed. Włodzimierz Bolecki, 163–166, Varia 2 (Kraków: Wydawnictwo Literackie, 2004); [Mieroszewski, Juliusz] Londyńczyk, "Gombrowicz w Berlinie," in *Polemiki i dyskusje*, ed. Włodzimierz Bolecki, 188–190, Varia 2 (Kraków: Wydawnictwo Literackie, 2004); [Mieroszewski, Juliusz] Londyńczyk, "Renesans w Pełni," in *Polemiki i dyskusje*, ed. Włodzimierz Bolecki, Varia 2 (Kraków: Wydawnictwo Literackie, 2004).
14 See the correspondence between Gombrowicz and Giedroyc: Witold Gombrowicz and Jerzy Giedroyc, *Listy 1950–1969*, ed. Andrzej S. Kowalczyk (Warszawa: Spółdzielnia Wydawnicza „Czytelnik," 2006), 544–570.
15 Among those who attacked Gombrowicz were Stanisław Zieliński, Jan Hieronim Morstin, and Krzysztof T. Toeplitz. Ludwik H. Morstin, "List do Gombrowicza," in *Polemiki i dyskusje*, ed. Włodzimierz Bolecki, 160–163, Varia 2 (Kraków: Wydawnictwo Literackie, 2004); Stanisław Zieliński, "Posłuchajcie Jeleńskiego,"

in *Polemiki i dyskusje*, ed. Włodzimierz Bolecki, 179–181, Varia 2 (Kraków: Wydawnictwo Literackie, 2004); Krzysztof T. Toeplitz, "Szlachetność Plotki," in *Polemiki i dyskusje*, ed. Włodzimierz Bolecki, 193–197, Varia 2 (Kraków: Wydawnictwo Literackie, 2004). The echo of the communist intrigue is to be found in the longer study on Gombrowicz published by Artur Sandauer in 1965: Artur Sandauer, "Witold Gombrowicz – człowiek i pisarz," in *Zebrane pisma krytyczne: Studia o literaturze współczesnej*, 3 vols., 581–613 1 (Państwowy Instytut Wydawniczy, 1981).

16 Joanna Siedlecka, "Gombrowicz w sieci Bezpieki," *Rzeczpospolita: Plus Minus*, December 4, 2010, http://www.rp.pl/artykul/573405-Gombrowicz-w-sieci-bezpieki-.html&cid=44&template=restricted (accessed January 8, 2018); Klementyna Suchanow, *Gombrowicz: Ja, geniusz*, 2 vols. (Wołowiec: Wydawnictwo Czarne, 2017), II 298-300; II 303–319.

17 Gasyna, "Rituals at the Limits of Literature,": 1323.

18 Maja Kittel, "Dlaczego Gombrowicz wolał Schopenhauera od Kanta?," *Przegląd Filozoficzno-Literacki* 10, no. 4 (2001): 147; Robert Boyers, "Gombrowicz' *Cosmos*: The Clinical Fiction as a Novel," *Principles of Psychology: Human Inquiries* XI, 1–2 (1971): 18.

19 Jerzy Jarzębski, "Gombrowicz i natura," *Teksty Drugie*, no. 3 (2005): 24–5; Boyers, "Gombrowicz' *Cosmos*,": 13.

20 Konstanty A. Jeleński, "[Wspomnienie, 1984]," in *Gombrowicz w Europie: Świadectwa i dokumenty 1963–1969*, ed. Rita Gombrowicz, 17–32 (Kraków: Wydawnictwo Literackie, 2002), 23.

21 Gasyna, "Rituals at the Limits of Literature,": 1330.

22 Danuta Borchardt, "Translator's Note," in *Cosmos*, vii–ix (New Haven: Yale University Press, 2005), viii.

23 It means selfish adhering to personal matters or affairs and not disturbing others.

24 On the role of compulsions in the onanist contexts in *Cosmos*, see: Boyers, "Gombrowicz' *Cosmos*,": 8–9.

25 Jarzębski, "Gombrowicz i natura,": 23, 25.

26 Quoted in: John Gray, *Feline Philosophy: Cats and the Meaning of Life* ([S.l.]: Penguin Books, 2021), 6.

27 Cf. Gombrowicz's half-ironical statement that "[i]n order to understand Nietzsche, it is necessary to understand an idea as simple as that of raising cows" (GP 101).

28 Paweł Mościcki, "Gombrowicz i nieludzkie," *Przegląd Filozoficzno-Literacki* 10, no. 4 (2001).

29 Cf. the study: Jarzębski, "Gombrowicz i natura."

30 Kittel, "Dlaczego Gombrowicz wolał Schopenhauera od Kanta?"

31 Arthur Schopenhauer, *The Two Fundamental Problems of Ethics*, with the assistance of David E. Cartwright, and Edward E. Erdmann (Oxford, New York: Oxford University Press, 2010), 233–234.

32 Ibid., 242.

33 Ibid., 234.

34 Kittel, "Dlaczego Gombrowicz wolał Schopenhauera od Kanta?,": 153. Cf. in that context Agata Bielik-Robson's parallel between Gombrowicz and Nietzsche: Agata Bielik-Robson, "Gombrowicz rzeźnik: mięsem w strukturę: Gombrowicz o filozofii, francuskiej zwłaszcza," in *Gdzie wschodzi Gombrowicz i kędy zapada*, ed. Aleksander Zbrzezny and Jakub Mach, 15–20 (Warszawa: Wydział Filozofii i Socjologii Uniwersytetu Warszawskiego, 2004), 17.

35 Monika Żółkoś, "Gombrowicz w świecie zwierząt," *Dialog* 651, no. 2 (2011): 140; Czesław Miłosz, "Przyrodnik," *Miesięcznik ZNAK* 579, no. 8 (2003): 19.

36 Włodzimierz Bolecki, "'Jak zachować się wobec krowy?': (Wstęp do *Bestiarium* Witolda Gombrowicza)," in *Bestiarium*, ed. Włodzimierz Bolecki, 7–18 (Kraków: Wydawnictwo Literackie, 2004), 18.

37 Gombrowicz's attitude toward Roman Catholicism was skeptical (as it was toward any other finite and closed worldview), but he appreciated its pessimistic anthropology (see D 36–37). But as early as 1944, in a short essay first published in Spanish, he points out that Catholicism as a philosophy deals with outdated topics and should be preparing for a "new battle": Witold Gombrowicz, "Katolicyzm wobec nowych prądów w sztuce," in *Czytelnicy i krytycy: Proza, reportaże, krytyka literacka, eseje, przedmowy*, ed. Włodzimierz Bolecki, 324–328, Varia 1 (Kraków: Wydawnictwo Literackie, 2004).

38 As Gombrowicz notes, Marxism objects to the exploitation of humans, but accepts (or raises no concerns about) the exploitation of animals (D 318). Żołkoś, "Gombrowicz w świecie zwierząt,": 141.

39 Błoński, *Forma, śmiech i rzeczy ostateczne*, 274–278. Cf. the remark in *Diary* from the year 1966: "In the sixty-first year of my life I have attained what a man usually acquires around thirty: a family life, apartment, dog, cat, comforts… And I have undoubtedly also become (everything testifies to this) a 'writer'" (D 673).

7 Epilogue

Taking into consideration Gombrowicz's skeptical attitude toward any pompousness, especially in combination with any state celebration of artists, writers, and other "great representatives of our nation," the official centenary of his birth in Poland was quite a paradox. The year 2004, was officially designated "The Witold Gombrowicz Year" and was celebrated in a grand manner by the entire nation, with new publications, symposia, and public gatherings. One could feel at the time that Gombrowicz, thanks to his critiques of a simplistic, nationalist understanding of Polishness, and pleas for an individualistic appreciation of sexuality and youth, served as a profound inspiration for the notion that one could successfully embrace a cosmopolitan, transnational identity as a liberal ironist *made in Poland* and, moreover, even gain global acknowledgment as a writer and intellectual. The fact that the same year, Poland, along with nine other Central European countries, joined the European Union, stood in natural accordance with this optimistic approach. The year 2019, marking the fiftieth anniversary of Gombrowicz's death, was another thing altogether. Whereas the official state disregard of this anniversary can be attributed to the conservative and homophobic agenda of the Polish government at the time, one could also notice a growing indifference among the representatives of the other, progressive side of the cultural-political spectrum. Gombrowicz's works, although still diligently scrutinized by literary scholars and still keenly staged by theater directors all over the world, appear to be slowly losing their stimulating emancipatory appeal: "individualism" appears to closely border on "selfishness," and "privilege."[1] The famous opening of the *Diary*, "Monday: Me. Tuesday: Me. Wednesday: Me. Thursday: Me" (D 3), once deeply inspirational and refreshing, now started to look doubtful. Furthermore, the fact that in Gombrowicz's literary universe sexuality is so invariably intertwined with violence, social disparities, and inequalities (cf. Kneadus' fascination with farmhands in *Ferdydurke*) may raise suspicions for many contemporary readers.[2]

But perhaps the greatest potential to challenge the sensibilities of modern-day readers lies in Gombrowicz's unyielding rejection of collective sentiments related to identity, such as nationality, race, and gender. In societies

DOI: 10.4324/9781003183976-7

increasingly characterized by identity politics and the valorization of group identities, his insistence on individualism and the assertion of intellectual autarchy over any solidarity effectively test the popular conviction (deeply rooted in the broadly understood Christian culture) that suffering, especially suffering as a target of persecution or oppression, inherently leads to greater epistemological insight or even to moral superiority. Gombrowicz, in his writings, consistently questions any attempts to romanticize suffering and victimhood, showing experience of pain, death, and decay is senseless and because of its inevitability should be seen rather as a kind of metaphysical scandal. His work—similarly to the work of other great modernist authors, such as Hannah Arendt, Albert Camus, or Thomas Mann—thus invites its readers to constantly reevaluate the preconceived notions about the relationships between suffering, morality, and wisdom, leaving no space for comfort or relief. "Nothing," he wrote in 1953, "will absolve you of yourself" (D 71).

Notes

1 See the review of Klementyna Suchanow's biography by the leftist-liberal literary critic Kinga Dunin, entitled simply "Gombrowicz Was an Idiot" (Polish: *Gombrowicz był idiotą*): Kinga Dunin, "Gombrowicz był idiotą," *Krytyka Polityczna*, August 16, 2018, https://krytykapolityczna.pl/kultura/czytaj-dalej/kinga-dunin-czyta/gombrowicz-byl-idiota/ (accessed May 20, 2023).

2 More details on the differences between 2004 and 2019 in Gombrowicz's reception are presented in: Aleksandra Konarzewska, "Witold Gombrowicz, Again: Between Argentina and Germany," *Russian Literature* 120–121 (2021).

Calendarium

Year	*Historical events*	*Cultural contexts (publications' years)*	*Gombrowicz's life and work*
1901	Queen Victoria's death	Thomas Mann's *Buddenbrooks*	
1902		Joseph Conrad's *Heart of Darkness*	
1903		Thomas Mann's *Tonio Kröger*	
1904	Begin of constructions of the Panama Canal	Joseph Conrad's *Nostromo*	Birth in Małoszyce (Russian Empire) on 04.08.1904
1905	Revolution in the Russian Empire		Gombrowicz family moves to Bodzechów
1906			
1907		Henri Bergson's *Creative Evolution*	
1908	The Young Turk Revolution in the Ottoman Empire	Friedrich Nietzsche's *Ecce Homo: How One Becomes What One Is*	
1909			
1910			
1911		Joseph Conrad's *Under Western Eyes*	Gombrowicz family moves to Warsaw
1912	Beginning of the Balkan Wars (1912–1913)	Thomas Mann's *Death in Venice*	
1913		Marcel Proust's *Swann's Way*; Franz Kafka's *The Judgement*	
1914	Beginning of the First World War		

Year	*Historical events*	*Cultural contexts (publications' years)*	*Gombrowicz's life and work*
1915		Joseph Conrad's *Victory*; Franz Kafka's *The Metamorphosis*	First goes to school
1916	Hipólito Yrigoyen becomes Argentina's first democratically elected president		
1917	February and October Revolution in Russia	Joseph Conrad's *The Shadow Line*	
1918	End of the First World War; Poland regains independence in November 1918; November Revolution in Germany (1918–1919); start of the Red Terror (1918–1922) in Bolshevik Russia	Guillaume Apollinaire's *Calligrammes: Poems of Peace and War 1913–1916*	
1919	Treaty of St. Germain and of Versailles	Marcel Proust's *In the Shadow of Young Girls in Flower*	
1920	Beginning of the Polish–Bolshevik war	Sigmund Freud's *Beyond the Pleasure Principle*; Max Weber's *The Protestant Ethic and the Spirit of Capitalism*	
1921	Treaty in Riga between Poland and Soviet Russia		
1922	Joseph Stalin becomes the General Secretary of the Communist Party of the Soviet Union; Geneva Accord and acknowledgment of the Polish–German border in Silesia; Benito Mussolini becomes prime minister in Italy; dissolution of the Ottoman Empire	Sinclair Lewis' *Babbit*; James Joyce's *Ulysses*	Barely passes school-leaving exams (*matura*); enrolment at the Faculty of Law at the University of Warsaw
1923	International acknowledgment of the Eastern borders of Poland	Martin Buber's *I and Thou*	
1924	Vladimir Lenin's death	Thomas Mann's *The Magic Mountain*	
1925		Franz Kafka's *The Trial*	

Year	*Historical events*	*Cultural contexts (publications' years)*	*Gombrowicz's life and work*
1926	Józef Piłsudski's coup in Poland		
1927		Martin Heidegger's *Being and Time*	Graduation from the University of Warsaw
1928			Stay in Paris (1928–1929)
1929	The Wall Street Crash and beginning of the Great Depression	Martin Heidegger's *Kant and the Problem of Metaphysics*	
1930	Brazilian Revolution	Sigmund Freud's *Civilisation and Its Discontents*	Beginning of work in a court
1931			
1932	The Great Famine in Soviet Ukraine (1932–1933)	Louis-Ferdinand Céline's *Journey to the End of the Night*	
1933	Adolf Hitler becomes chancellor of Germany	Czesław Miłosz's *A Poem on Frozen Time*	Publication of the short story "The Drama of Mrs. and Mr. Baroness" (*Dramat baronostwa*) in *Polska zbrojna*; publication of his first book: the collection of short stories *Recollections of Adolescence* (later renamed to *Bacacay*)
1934		Bruno Schulz's *Cinnamon Shops*	Publication of the short story "From the Private Diary of Hieronim Poniżalski" (*Z diariusza prywatnego Hieronima Poniżalskiego*) in *Gazeta Polska*
1935	Introducing the Nuremberg Laws in Nazi Germany	Jorge L. Borges' *A Universal History of Infamy*	Publication of the short stories in various newspapers and magazines: "Notes (Mechanism of Life, Bureaucrat)" *(Uwagi [Mechanizm Życia, Biurokrata])*; "Apostrophe to Tośka" *(Apostrofa do Tośki)*; "Tośka (Fragments)" *(Tośka [Fragmenty])*; "The Well (A Grotesque)" *(Studnia [Groteska])*, writing the short story *"Ears"* (*Uszy*)

Year	*Historical events*	*Cultural contexts (publications' years)*	*Gombrowicz's life and work*
1936	Beginning of the Spanish Civil War (1936–1939) and of the Great Terror in Soviet Union (1936–1938)	Czesław Miłosz's *Three Winters*	
1937	*Polish Operation* of the NKVD (1937–1938) in the Soviet Union	Bruno Schulz' *Sanatorium Under the Sign of the Hourglass*	Publication of the novel *Ferdydurke;* publication of the short story "Pampelan in a Tube" (*Pampelan w tubie*)
1938	Germany's "Anschluss" of Austria; The Munich Agreement (30.09.1938) and annexation of part of Czechoslovakia by Germany	Jean-Paul Sartre's *Nausea*	Publication of the play *Princess Ivona* in *Skamander*
1939	Germany's establishing the Protectorate of Bohemia and Moravia (14.03.1939); Nazi–Soviet non-aggression pact (23.08.1939); Germany's attack on Poland and the start of the Second World War in Europe (01.09.1939)		Publication of the short story "On the Kitchen Steps" (*Na kuchennych schodach*) in *Skamander* and the novel in episodes *Possessed* (*Opętani*, 1939); travel to South America in the summer of 1939 and decision to stay Argentina
1940	The Katyn Massacre		
1941	Germany's invasion of the Soviet Union; Japan's attack on Pearl Harbor	Vladimir Nabokov's *The Real Life of Sebastian Knight*	
1942	Nazi Wannsee Conference on the "Final Solution"	Albert Camus' *The Stranger* and *The Myth of Sisyphus*	
1943	The Warsaw Ghetto Uprising; coup d'état in Argentina; the Teheran Conference	Jean-Paul Sartre's *Being and Nothingness* and *The Flies*	
1944	The Warsaw Uprising	Jean-Paul Sartre's *No Exit*	
1945	The Yalta Conference; end of the Second World War in Europe (08.05.1945); Juan Perón's rise to power in Argentina (17.10.1945)		
1946		Jean-Paul Sartre's *Existentialism Is a Humanism*	

Year	*Historical events*	*Cultural contexts (publications' years)*	*Gombrowicz's life and work*
1947	Falsified legislative election in Poland	Martin Heidegger's *Letter on Humanism*; Jean-Paul Sartre's *What is Literature?*; Albert Camus' *The Plague*	Begin of work in Banco Polaco in Argentina; Argentinian edition of *Ferdydurke*
1948	Proclamation of the State of Israel	Martin Buber's *The Problem of Man*	Argentinian edition of *The Marriage*
1949	Proclamations of People's Republic of China, the Federal Republic of Germany, and the German Democratic Republic	Jean Genet's *The Thief's Journal*; Jorge L. Borges' *The Aleph and Other Stories*	
1950	Proclamation of the Republic of India		Beginning of contacts with Jerzy Giedroyc and Instytut Literacki in Paris
1951	Treaty of Paris (establishing the European Coal and Steel Community)	Albert Camus' *The Rebell;* Julio Cortázar's *Bestiario*	First publications in Giedroyc's journal *Kultura*: fragments of the novella *Trans-Atlantyk*, essay *Against Poets*, and *Fragments from Diary*
1952	Nationalization of key industries in Argentina, including railways and banks; July Constitution in Poland (introduction a new name: *Polska Rzeczpospolita Ludowa*, the Polish People's Republic)	Jean-Paul Sartre's *Saint Genet, Actor and Martyr*	Polemics with Emil Cioran published by *Kultura* (later included in *Diary*)
1953	Death of Joseph Stalin	Dionys Mascolo's *Le Communisme. Révolution et communication ou la dialectique des valeurs et des besoins*; Martin Buber's *Eclipse of God*; Czesław Miłosz's *The Captive Mind*	Short story *"Banquet"* (*Bankiet*) in *Wiadomości* (in London), the novel *Trans-Atlantyk*, and the play *The Marriage* (in one volume) published by Instytut Literacki in Paris
1954			
1955	Military coup in Argentina against Juan Perón (*Revolución Libertadora*, "Liberating Revolution")	Vladimir Nabokov's *Lolita*	Resigns from work in Banco Polaco

Year	*Historical events*	*Cultural contexts (publications' years)*	*Gombrowicz's life and work*
1956	Khrushchev's "Secret Speech" and beginning of the "Thaw" in the Soviet Union and the Eastern Block; "Polish October"; Soviet military intervention in Hungary	Albert Camus' *The Fall*	First volume of *Diary (1953–1956)* published by Instytut Literacki
1957	Treaty of Rome (establishing the European Economic Community)	Roland Barth's *Mythologies*	In Poland: publication of the collection of short stories *Bacacay* (based on *Recollections of Adolescence*), the novella *Trans-Atlantyk*, and the play *Marriage* (in one volume); reedition of the novel *Ferdydurke;* Halina Mikołajska's staging *Princess Ivona* in Warsaw
1958			In Poland: publication of the play *Princess Ivona* (as a book)
1959	The Cuban Revolution	Czesław Miłosz's *Native Realm*	
1960		Julio Cortázar's *The Winners*	Jerzy Jarocki's staging *The Marriage* in Gliwice (Silesia); novel *Pornografia* published by Instytut Literacki
1961	Construction of the Berlin Wall	Ernesto Sabato's *On Heroes and Tombs* (French edition in 1967 with a foreword by Witold Gombrowicz)	Publication of the English translation of *Ferdydurke*, French edition of *Pornografia,* and the German edition of *Diary*
1962	Cuban Missile Crisis	Claude Lévi-Strauss' *The Savage Mind*	Publication of the second volume of *Diary (1957–1961)* by Instytut Literacki
1963		Ernesto Sabato's *The Writer in the Catastrophe of our Time*; Julio Cortázar's *Hopscotch*	Moves back to Europe: scholarship from the Ford Foundation in West Berlin (1963–1964)

Year	*Historical events*	*Cultural contexts (publications' years)*	*Gombrowicz's life and work*
1964	"Letter of 34": letter by of Polish intellectuals protesting censorship and restrictions on the allocation of paper for books and magazines	Roland Barth's *Elements of Semiology*	Moving to France and settling in Vence (Southern France); Jorge Lavelli's staging of *The Marriage* in Paris
1965			Publication of the novel *Cosmos* in Instytut Literacki; Alf Sjöberg's staging of *Princess Ivona Marriage* in Stockholm
1966	Cultural Revolution in People's Republic of China (1966–1976)	Michael Foucault's *The Order of Things: An Archaeology of the Human Sciences*	Third volume of *Diary (1962–1966)* published in one volume together with *Operetta* by Instytut Literacki
1967	Six-Day War in Israel	Jacques Derrida's *Of Grammatology*	The International Prix Formentor Award (Formentor Literature Prize)
1968	Prague Spring; students' revolt in Western Europe and United States; Warsaw Pact military intervention in Czechoslovakia		French edition of the *Testament* (as *Entretiens avec Witold Gombrowicz*); marriage to Rita Labrosse
1969		Michael Foucault's *Archaeology of Knowledge*	Polish edition of the *Testament* published by Instytut Literacki; working on lectures on philosophy (published posthumously as *A Guide to Philosophy in Six Hours and Fifteen Minutes*); death in Vence on 24.07.1969

Bibliography

Archive materials and edited sources

[Letters to "Kultura" concerning Witold Gombrowicz], 1951–1967, GEN MSS 515 Box 35 f. 1016, Witold Gombrowicz Archive, Beinecke Rare Book and Manuscript Library, Yale University.

"33 Schriftsteller Nennen Ihre Literarischen Leitbilder." *Tagesblatt* (25.12.1960), GEN MSS 515 Box 16 f. 549, Witold Gombrowicz Archive, Beinecke Rare Book and Manuscript Library, Yale University, 1960.

Bergman, Ingmar. *[Letter]*, November 2, 1964, GEN MSS 515 Box 1 f. 28, Witold Gombrowicz Archive, Beinecke Rare Book and Manuscript Library, Yale University.

Buber, Martin. *[Letter]*, July 9, 1951, GEN MSS 515 Box 2 f. 52, Witold Gombrowicz Archive, Beinecke Rare Book and Manuscript Library, Yale University.

Cataluccio, Francesco M., and Jerzy Illg, eds. *Gombrowicz filozof.* Kraków: Społeczny Instytut Wydawniczy Znak, 1991.

Gombrowicz, Rita, ed. *Gombrowicz w Argentynie: Świadectwa i dokumenty 1939–1963.* Kraków: Wydawnictwo Literackie, 2004.

Gombrowicz, Rita, ed. *Gombrowicz w Europie: Świadectwa i dokumenty 1963–1969.* Kraków: Wydawnictwo Literackie, 2002.

Gombrowicz, Witold, François Bondy, Konstanty A. Jeleński, and Dominique d. Roux. *Gombrowicz: Walka o sławę* (2). Edited by Jerzy Jarzębski. Kraków: Wydawnictwo Literackie, 1998.

Gombrowicz, Witold, and Jean Dubuffet. *Korespondencja.* Kraków: Wydawnictwo Literackie, 2005.

Gombrowicz, Witold, and Jerzy Giedroyc. *Listy 1950–1969.* Edited by Andrzej S. Kowalczyk. Warszawa: Spółdzielnia Wydawnicza „Czytelnik", 2006.

Gombrowicz, Witold, Jarosław Iwaszkiewicz, Artur Sandauer, and Józef Wittlin. *Gombrowicz: Walka o sławę* (1). Edited by Jerzy Jarzębski. Kraków: Wydawnictwo Literackie, 1996.

Gombrowicz, Witold, and Czesław Miłosz. *Konfrontacje.* Edited by Michał Szymański and Barbara Toruńczyk. Warszawa: Zeszyty Literackie, 2015.

Gombrowicz, Witold. *[Letters to Czeslaw Milosz from Witold Gombrowicz]*, 1954–1969, GEN MSS 661 Box 21 f. 350, Czesław Miłosz Papers, Beinecke Rare Book and Manuscript Library, Yale University.

Gombrowicz, Witold. *Bestiarium.* Edited by Włodzimierz Bolecki. Kraków: Wydawnictwo Literackie, 2004.

Gombrowicz, Witold. *Czytelnicy i krytycy: Proza, reportaże, krytyka literacka, eseje, przedmowy*. Edited by Włodzimierz Bolecki. *Varia* 1. Kraków: Wydawnictwo Literackie, 2004.

Gombrowicz, Witold. *Jak czytają Gombrowicza w kraju ('Ferdydurke', 'Dziennik'); Krótka historia 'Ferdydurke' [Publicity material in Polish, typescript carbon, typescript annotated (photocopy)/n.d.]*, n.d., GEN MSS 515 Box 12 f. 448, Witold Gombrowicz Archive, Beinecke Rare Book and Manuscript Library, Yale University.

Gombrowicz, Witold. *Kronika Ferdydurke [notes about the reception of Ferdydurke]*, 1947, GEN MSS 515 Box 12 f. 445, Witold Gombrowicz Archive, Beinecke Rare Book and Manuscript Library, Yale University.

Gombrowicz, Witold. *Kronos*. Edited by Rita Gombrowicz, Jerzy Jarzębski, and Klementyna Suchanow. Kraków: Wydawnictwo Literackie, 2013.

Gombrowicz, Witold. *List do Ferdydurkistów: Wywiady, odpowiedzi na ankiety, listy do redakcji czasopism*. Edited by Włodzimierz Bolecki. *Varia* 3. Kraków: Wydawnictwo Literackie, 2004.

Gombrowicz, Witold. *Operetka [IV] [typescript, carbon, corrected]*, 1966, GEN MSS 515 Box 15 f. 534, Witold Gombrowicz Archive, Beinecke Rare Book and Manuscript Library, Yale University.

Gombrowicz, Witold. *Polemiki i dyskusje*. Edited by Włodzimierz Bolecki. *Varia* 2. Kraków: Wydawnictwo Literackie, 2004.

Gombrowicz, Witold. *Testament: Rozmowy z Dominique de Roux*. With the assistance of Dominique d. Roux. Kraków: Wydawnictwo Literackie, 1996.

Monographs and collected volumes

Anders, Jaroslaw. *Between Fire and Sleep: Essays on Modern Polish Literature*. New Haven: Yale University Press, 2009.

Arendt, Hannah. *Rahel Varnhagen: Lebensgeschichte einer deutschen Jüdin aus der Romantik*. München: Piper, 1959.

Arendt, Hannah, and Gershom Scholem. *The Correspondence of Hannah Arendt and Gershom Scholem*. Edited by Marie L. Knott and Anthony David. Chicago: University of Chicago Press, 2017.

Benjamin, Walter. *Das Kunstwerk im Zeitalter seiner technischen Reproduzierbarkeit*. Frankfurt/Main: Suhrkamp, 2010.

Błoński, Jan. *Forma, śmiech i rzeczy ostateczne: studia o Gombrowiczu*. Kraków: Towarzystwo Autorów i Wydawców Prac Naukowych Universitas, 2003.

Boy-Żeleński, Tadeusz. *Reflektorem w mrok: wybór publicystyki*. Edited by Andrzej Z. Makowiecki. Warszawa: Państwowy Instytut Wydawniczy, 1985.

Brzozowski, Stanisław. *Der Geschichtsmaterialismus als Kulturphilosophie und andere Schriften*. Edited by Aleksandra Konarzewska and Alexander K. Golec. Stuttgart: Ibidem Verlag, 2021.

Buber, Martin. *Schriften zu Philosophie und Religion*. Edited by Ashraf Noor and Kerstin Schreck. Martin Buber Werkausgabe Band 12. Gütersloh: Gütersloher Verlagshaus, 2017.

Camus, Albert. *The Stranger*. With the assistance of Matthew Ward. New York: Vintage International, 1989.

Dapía, Silvia G. ed. *Gombrowicz in Transnational Context: Translation, Affect, and Politics*. New York: Routledge, 2019.

Etkind, Alexander. *Internal Colonization: Russia's Imperial Experience*. Cambridge, Malden: Polity Press, 2011.

Fanning, David, and Erik Levi, eds. *The Routledge Handbook to Music Under German Occupation, 1938–1945: Propaganda, Myth and Reality*. Routledge Handbooks Online. Abingdon: Routledge, 2019.

Gall, Alfred. *Performativer Humanismus: Die Auseinandersetzung mit Philosophie in der literarischen Praxis von Witold Gombrowicz*. Dresden: Thelem, 2007.

Garbal, Łukasz. *Ferdydurke: biografia powieści*. Kraków: Towarzystwo Autorów i Wydawców Prac Naukowych "Universitas," 2010.

Girard, René. *Deceit, Desire, and the Novel: Self and Other in Literary Structure*. Baltimore: Johns Hopkins University Press, 1976.

Głowiński, Michał. *Gombrowicz i nadliteratura*. Kraków: Wydawnictwo Literackie, 2002.

Gray, John. *Feline Philosophy: Cats and the Meaning of Life*. [S.l.]: Penguin Books, 2021.

Gutthy, Agnieszka, ed. *Literature in Exile of East and Central Europe*. New York: Peter Lang, 2009.

Ingarden, Roman. *Das literarische Kunstwerk: Eine Untersuchung aus dem Grenzgebiet der Ontologie, Logik und Literaturwissenschaft*. Halle (Saale): M. Niemeyer, 1931.

Jarzębski, Jerzy. *Gra w Gombrowicza*. Warszawa: Państwowy Instytut Wydawniczy, 1982.

Jaszewska, Dagmara. *Nasza niedojrzała kultura: Postmodernizm inspirowany Gombrowiczem*. Warszawa: Oficyna Naukowa, 2002.

Jeleński, Konstanty A. *Chwile oderwane*. Edited by Piotr Kłoczowski. Gdańsk: słowo/obraz terytoria, 2010.

Karpiński, Wojciech. *Książki zbójeckie*. Warszawa: Zeszyty Literackie, 2009.

Kobyłecka-Piwońska, Ewa. *Spojrzenia z zewnątrz: Witold Gombrowicz w literaturze argentyńskiej (1970–2017)*. Łódź: Wydawnictwo Uniwersytetu Łódzkiego, 2017.

Konarzewska, Aleksandra. *Der Ausgang sus der Unmündigkeit: Sexualität, Kultivierung und Entzauberung der Welt in der Prosa von Stanisław Brzozowski und Witold Gombrowicz*. Frankfurt a.M: Peter Lang, 2020.

Łapiński, Zdzisław, ed. *Gombrowicz i krytycy*. Kraków, Wrocław: Wydawnictwo Literackie, 1984.

Lavrinenko, Yurii, ed. *Rozstriliane Vidrodzhennia: Antolohiia 1917–1933: Poeziia—Proza—Drama—Esei*. Biblioteka "Kultury" XXXVII. Paryż: Instytut Literacki, 1959. https://staticnowyportal.kulturaparyska.com/attachments/51/58/1c83543de7383cf82472ec5ea5a3d67a0f7be0f9.pdf (accessed March 1, 2023).

Lawaty, Andreas, and Marek Zybura, eds. *Gombrowicz in Europa: Deutsch-Polnische Versuche einer kulturellen Verortung*. Wiesbaden: Harrassowitz, 2006.

Legierski, Michał. *Modernizm Witolda Gombrowicza*. Warszawa: Instytut Badań Literackich Polskiej Akademii Nauk, 1999.

Mann, Thomas. *Death in Venice*. With the assistance of Michael H. Heim. [s. l.]: Ecco, 2004.

Mann, Thomas. *Frühe Erzählungen 1893–1912: In der Fassung der Großen kommentierten Frankfurter Ausgabe*. Frankfurt am Main: Fischer Taschenbuch Verlag, 2008.

Markowski, Michał P. *Czarny nurt: Gombrowicz, świat, literatura*. Kraków: Wydawnictwo Literackie, 2004.

Miłosz, Czesław. *Przygody młodego umysłu: Publicystyka i proza 1931–1939*. Edited by Agnieszka Stawiarska. Kraków: Społeczny Instytut Wydawniczy Znak, 2003.

Miłosz, Czesław. *Rok myśliwego*. Kraków: Społeczny Instytut Wydawniczy Znak, 2001.

Nietzsche, Friedrich W. *On the Genealogy of Morality*. Edited by Keith Ansell-Pearson. Cambridge, New York: Cambridge University Press, 2007.

Nowak, Tomasz. *Polski, polonez, chodzony*. Roczyny: Fundacja „MEMO", 2018.

Nycz, Ryszard. *Sylwy współczesne*. Kraków: Towarzystwo Autorów i Wydawców Prac Naukowych Universitas, 1996.

Salgas, Jean-Pierre. *Witold Gombrowicz ou l'athéisme généralisé*. Paris: Édition du Seuil, 2000.

Schopenhauer, Arthur. *The Two Fundamental Problems of Ethics*. With the assistance of David E. Cartwright, and Edward E. Erdmann. Oxford, New York: Oxford University Press, 2010.

Schopenhauer, Arthur. *The World as Will and Representation*. With the assistance of E. F. J. Payne. 2 vols. New York: Dover Publications, 1969.

Siedlecka, Joanna. *Jaśniepanicz: O Witoldzie Gombrowiczu*. Kraków: Wydawnictwo Literackie, 1987.

Snyder, Timothy. *Bloodlands: Europe Between Hitler and Stalin*. New York: Basic Books, 2010.

Starosta, Anita. *Form and Instability: Eastern Europe, Literature, Postimperial Difference*. Evanston: Northwestern University Press, 2016.

Suchanow, Klementyna. *Gombrowicz: Ja, geniusz*. 2 vols. Wołowiec: Wydawnictwo Czarne, 2017.

Szpakowska, Małgorzata. *„Wiadomości literackie" Prawie dla wszystkich*. Warszawa: Wydawnictwo W.A.B, 2012.

Szymborska, Wisława. *Nic dwa razy/Nothing Twice: Wybór wierszy/Selected Poems*. With the assistance of Stanisław Barańczak, and Clare Cavanagh. Kraków: Wydawnictwo Literackie, 2012.

Thompson, Ewa M. *Witold Gombrowicz*. Boston: Twayne Publishers, 1979.

Trojanowska, Tamara, Joanna Niżyńska, Przemysław Czapliński, and Agnieszka Polakowska, eds. *Being Poland: A New History of Polish Literature and Culture Since 1918*. Toronto: University of Toronto Press, 2019.

Zbrzezny, Aleksander, and Jakub Mach, eds. *Gdzie wschodzi Gombrowicz i kędy zapada*. Warszawa: Wydział Filozofii i Socjologii Uniwersytetu Warszawskiego, 2004.

Zybura, Marek, ed. *Ein Patagonier in Berlin: Texte der deutschen Gombrowicz-Rezeption*. Dresden: Neisse Verlag, 2018.

Articles and book chapters

"Czasami skakałam w kosmos: [Interview with Barbara Krafft-Seidner]." *Rzeczpospolita* (02.12.2008). https://www.rp.pl/teatr/art7925741-czasami-skakalam-w-kosmos (accessed May 18, 2021).

Balderston, Daniel. "Rex Café, Buenos Aires, 1947: On the Spanish Translation of Gombrowicz's *Ferdydurke*." *The Polish Review* 60, no. 2 (2015): 29.

Barilli, Renato. "Sartre i Camus w dzienniku." In *Gombrowicz filozof*. Edited by Francesco M. Cataluccio and Jerzy Illg, 227–239. Kraków: Społeczny Instytut Wydawniczy Znak, 1991.

Berressem, Hanjo. "Witold Gombrowicz: 'Cosmos' the Case of the Hanged Sparrow." *The Polish Review* 36, no. 2 (1991): 145–159.

Bhambry, Tul'si. "'The Quieter the Louder Indeed': Silence and the Space of Literature in *Trans-Atlantyk*." In *Gombrowicz in Transnational Context: Translation, Affect, and Politics*. Edited by Silvia G. Dapía, 154–168. New York: Routledge, 2019.

Bielik-Robson, Agata. "Gombrowicz rzeźnik: mięsem w strukturę: Gombrowicz o filozofii, francuskiej zwłaszcza." In *Gdzie wschodzi Gombrowicz i kędy zapada*. Edited by Aleksander Zbrzezny and Jakub Mach, 15–20. Warszawa: Wydział Filozofii i Socjologii Uniwersytetu Warszawskiego, 2004.

Bolecki, Włodzimierz. "A Concise Companion to Polish Modernism." In *Being Poland: A New History of Polish Literature and Culture since 1918*. Edited by Tamara Trojanowska et al., 105–131. Toronto: University of Toronto Press, 2019.

Bolecki, Włodzimierz. "Gombrowicz and Science." *Russian Literature* 62, no. 4 (2007): 389–400.

Bolecki, Włodzimierz. "'Jak zachować się wobec krowy?': (Wstęp do bestiarium Witolda Gombrowicza)." In *Bestiarium*. Edited by Włodzimierz Bolecki, 7–18. Kraków: Wydawnictwo Literackie, 2004.

Bolecki, Włodzimierz. "Słowacki Gombrowicza." *Teksty Drugie* 121–122, 1–2 (2007): 171–192.

Borchardt, Danuta. "Translator's Note." In *Cosmos*, vii–ix. New Haven: Yale University Press, 2005.

Boyers, Robert. "Aspects of the Perverse in Gombrowicz' Pornografia." *Salmagundi*, no. 17 (1971): 18–46.

Boyers, Robert. "Gombrowicz' Cosmos: The Clinical Fiction as a Novel." *Principles of Psychology: Human Inquiries* XI, 1–2 (1971): 1–24.

Brodsky, David. "Witold Gombrowicz and the 'Polish October'." *Slavic Review* 39, no. 3 (1980): 459–475.

Cataluccio, Francesco M. "Gombrowicz filozof." In *Gombrowicz filozof*. Edited by Francesco M. Cataluccio and Jerzy Illg, 5–24. Kraków: Społeczny Instytut Wydawniczy Znak, 1991.

Chwin, Stefan. "Grzechy Gombrowicza przeciwko wolności: O projekcie etycznym wpisanym w 'Ferdydurke'." *Przestrzenie Teorii*, no. 20 (2013): 11–27.

Dapía, Silvia G. "'Living in Another Language': Witold Gombrowicz's Argentinean Experience." *Polish American Studies* 71, no. 2 (2014): 79–89.

Dapía, Silvia G. "The Anatomy of Feeling in Gombrowicz's 'A Premeditated Crime' ('Zbrodnia z premedytacją')." In *Gombrowicz in Transnational Context: Translation, Affect, and Politics*. Edited by Silvia G. Dapía, 169–184. New York: Routledge, 2019.

Dapía, Silvia G. "The First Poststructuralist: Gombrowicz's Debt to Nietzsche." *The Polish Review* 54, no. 1 (2009): 87–99.

Dauksza, Agnieszka. "Ciążąca (nie)obecność: Gombrowicz wobec wojny i Żydów." *Teksty Drugie*, no. 2 (2016): 211–230.

Dunin, Kinga. "Gombrowicz był idiotą." *Krytyka Polityczna*, August 16, 2018. https://krytykapolityczna.pl/kultura/czytaj-dalej/kinga-dunin-czyta/gombrowicz-byl-idiota/ (accessed May 20, 2023).

Eörsi, István. "Mój czas z Gombrowiczem." *Literatura na Świecie* 357, no. 4 (2001): 86–113.

Filipowicz, Halina. "Fission and Fusion: Polish Émigré Literature." *Slavic and East European Journal* 33, no. 2 (1989): 157–172.

Fiut, Aleksander. "Gombrowicz the First Post-Colonialist?" *Russian Literature* 62, no. 4 (2007): 433–439.

Fryde, Ludwik. "O 'Ferdydurke' Gombrowicza." In *Gombrowicz i krytycy*. Edited by Zdzisław Łapiński, 57–69. Kraków, Wrocław: Wydawnictwo Literackie, 1984.

Gamerro, Carlos. "The 'Puto' in Argentine Literature." In *Gombrowicz in Transnational Context: Translation, Affect, and Politics*. Edited by Silvia G. Dapía, 39–52. New York: Routledge, 2019.

Gasyna, George. "A Kind of Testament: Reading Witold Gombrowicz as a Transnational Writer." In *A Companion to World Literature*. Edited by Ken Seigneurie, 1–10. Hoboken: Wiley, 2020.

Gasyna, George. "Rituals at the Limits of Literature: A New Reading of Witold Gombrowicz's Cosmos." *The Sarmatian Review*, no. 3 (2007): 1323–1332.

Gasyna, George. "Toward Heterotopia: The Case of 'Trans-Atlantyk'." *Slavic Review* 68, no. 4 (2009): 898–923.

Głowiński, Michał. "Gombrowiczowska diatryba." *Pamiętnik Literacki*, no. 4 (2000): 63–81.

Goldmann, Lucien. "The Theatre of Gombrowicz." *The Drama Review: TDR* 14, no. 3 (1970): 102–112.

Gómez, Juan C. "Nowy przewodnik po Gombrowiczu." *Twórczość* 702, no. 5 (2004): 48–101.

Gömöri, George. "The Antinomies of Gombrowicz." *The Modern Language Review* 73, no. 1 (1978): 119–129.

Grimstad, Knut A. "What Jews Meant to Witold Gombrowicz, or: Philosemitism as a Strategy for Identity Formation." *The Slavonic and East European Review* 95, no. 4 (2017): 625–647.

Grinberg, Miguel. "Gombrowicz in Love." *Literatura na Świecie* 357, no. 4 (2001): 83–85.

Holmgren, Beth. "Witold Gombrowicz Within the *Wieszcz* Tradition." *The Slavic and East European Journal* 33, no. 4 (1989): 556–570.

Iribarne, Louis. "Revolution in the Theater of Witkacy and Gombrowicz." *The Polish Review* 18, no. 1/2 (1973): 58–76.

Jarzębski, Jerzy. "Gombrowicz i Natura." *Teksty Drugie*, no. 3 (2005): 17–26.

Jarzębski, Jerzy. "Gombrowicz i Szekspir." *Pamiętnik Literacki* CV, no. 3 (2014): 79–91.

Jarzębski, Jerzy. "Gombrowicz's Wild Youth: The 'Ferdydurkean Individual' Fades Away." In *Gombrowicz in Transnational Context: Translation, Affect, and Politics*. Edited by Silvia G. Dapía, 187–207. New York: Routledge, 2019.

Jativa, Tomasz. "Form and Power: On the Disciplinary Coding of National Identity in "Pamiętnik Stefana Czarnieckiego" by Witold Gombrowicz." *Czytanie Literatury. Łódzkie Studia Literaturoznawcze*, no. 9 (2020): 253–267.

Jeleński, Konstanty A. "Bohaterskie niebohaterstwo Gombrowicza." In *Chwile oderwane*. Edited by Piotr Kłoczowski, 35–50. Gdańsk: słowo/obraz terytoria, 2010.

Jeleński, Konstanty A. "Dział wód." In *Chwile oderwane*. Edited by Piotr Kłoczowski, 92–95. Gdańsk: słowo/obraz terytoria, 2010.

Just, Daniel. "The Difficult Childhood of an Adult: Aging and Maturity in Witold Gombrowicz's Pornografia." *Russian Literature* 116 (2020): 17–39.

Karpiński, Wojciech. "Głos Gombrowicza." In *Książki zbójeckie*, 141–159. Warszawa: Zeszyty Literackie, 2009.

Kittel, Maja. "Dlaczego Gombrowicz wolał Schopenhauera od Kanta?" *Przegląd Filozoficzno-Literacki* 10, no. 4 (2001): 131–153.

Konarzewska, Aleksandra. "Witold Gombrowicz, Again: Between Argentina and Germany." *Russian Literature* 120–121 (2021): 263–271.

Kopciński, Jacek. "Drama as a Manifold Portrait: Polish Drama After the Second World War." In *Being Poland: A New History of Polish Literature and Culture since 1918*. Edited by Tamara Trojanowska et al., 535–569. Toronto: University of Toronto Press, 2019.

Kowalczyk, Andrzej S. "'Their Astounding Strength in Overcoming Their Past…': The Memory of Nazism in the Berlin *Diary*." In *Gombrowicz in Transnational Context: Translation, Affect, and Politics*. Edited by Silvia G. Dapía, 208–224. New York: Routledge, 2019.

Kraszewski, Charles. "Neither the Forest nor the Trees: Witold Gombrowicz's *Pornografia*: Failed Novel or Cynical Masterpiece?" *The Polish Review* 50, no. 1 (2005): 41–67.

Kühl, Olaf. "Ciało i jego maskowanie u Gombrowicza." *Teksty Drugie* 37, no. 1 (1996): 59–68.

Łagowski, Bronisław. "Inny Gombrowicz." In *Gombrowicz filozof*. Edited by Francesco M. Cataluccio and Jerzy Illg, 168–176. Kraków: Społeczny Instytut Wydawniczy Znak, 1991.

Lutsky, Klara. "Living on the Margins and Loving It: Gombrowicz and Exile." In *Literature in Exile of East and Central Europe*. Edited by Agnieszka Gutthy, 73–87. New York: Peter Lang, 2009.

Lutsky, Klara. ""I Know What I Am Not": The Problem of the Marginal Self in Gombrowicz's Novels." *The Polish Review* 60, no. 2 (2015): 21–28.

Maciuszko, George J. "[Review]." *Books Abroad* 35, no. 3 (1961): 303.

Margański, Janusz. "Filozof Gombrowicz." *Teksty Drugie* 11, no. 5 (1991): 106–118.

Margański, Janusz. "Gombrowicz i muzyczność." *Teksty Drugie*, no. 3 (2005): 58–65.

Margański, Janusz. "Między powiastką a filozofią: O „Ferdydurke "Witolda Gombrowicza." *Pamiętnik Literacki*, no. 1 (2000): 125–139.

Markiewicz, Henryk. "Do genezy „Ferdydurke"." *Teksty Drugie* 6 (2004): 232–233.

Markowski, Michał P. "'Indomitable Boredom Above the Entire World': Gombrowicz (and Other Polish Writers) on Existential Predicament." In *Gombrowicz in Transnational Context: Translation, Affect, and Politics*. Edited by Silvia G. Dapía, 97–114. New York: Routledge, 2019.

Markowski, Michał P. "Ze szkoły Montaigne'a." In *Kurs filozofii w sześć godzin i kwadrans*, 5–12. Kraków: Wydawnictwo Literackie, 2017.

Merivale, Patricia. "The Esthetics of Perversion: Gothic Artifice in Henry James and Witold Gombrowicz." *PMLA* 93, no. 5 (1978): 992–1002.

Miłosz, Czesław. "Przyrodnik." *Miesięcznik ZNAK* 579, no. 8 (2003): 13–25.

Miłosz, Czesław. "Who Is Gombrowicz?" *Performing Arts Journal* 6, no. 3 (1982): 7–22.

Mościcki, Paweł. "Gombrowicz i nieludzkie." *Przegląd Filozoficzno-Literacki* 10, no. 4 (2001): 63–85.

Naliwajek, Katarzyna. "Nazi Musical Imperialism in Occupied Poland." In *The Routledge Handbook to Music under German Occupation, 1938–1945: Propaganda,*

Myth and Reality. Edited by David Fanning and Erik Levi. Routledge Handbooks Online. Abingdon: Routledge, 2019. https://www.routledgehandbooks.com/doi/10.4324/9781315230610-4.

Oklot, Michal. "Gombrowicz's *Kronos*: The Pornography of Aging." *Slavonica* 19, no. 2 (2014): 105–127.

Pasolini, Pier P. "Witold Gombrowicz, Diario 1957–61." In *Tutte le opere: Saggi sulla letteratura e sull'arte*. Edited by Walter Siti and Silvia de Laude, 1712–1772. Milano: Mondadori, 1999.

Piechura, Joanna, and Piotr Sadzik. "Maranizm pozwala na rewolucyjną i kompleksową rewizję polskiej kultury: [Rozmowa Joanny Piechury Z Piotrem Sadzikiem].". *Krytyka Polityczna*. https://krytykapolityczna.pl/kultura/czytaj-dalej/maranizm-w-literaturze-polskiej-rozmowa-joanny-piechury-z-piotrem-sadzikiem/ (accessed April 19, 2023).

Piglia, Ricardo. "¿Existe La Novela Argentina? Borges Y Gombrowicz." *Espacios de crítica y producción*, no. 6 (1987): 13–15. https://piglia.pubpub.org/pub/nx14ji96/release/1 (accessed January 18, 2022).

Pratt, Daniel. "Affect and Youth: Reading Gombrowicz with Deleuze." In *Gombrowicz in Transnational Context: Translation, Affect, and Politics*. Edited by Silvia G. Dapía, 142–153. New York: Routledge, 2019.

Pratt, Daniel. "Freddy Durkee and 'Ferdydurke': A Gombrowiczian Reading of 'Babbitt'." *Comparative Literature Studies* 52, no. 3 (2015): 562–584.

Pratt, Daniel. "Narrative and Form: Gombrowicz and the Narrative Conception of Personal Identity." *The Polish Review* 60, no. 2 (2015): 7–20.

Reichardt, Dieter. "Gombrowicz Vs. Borges." In *Gombrowicz in Europa: Deutsch-polnische Versuche einer kulturellen Verortung*. Edited by Andreas Lawaty and Marek Zybura, 17–28. Wiesbaden: Harrassowitz, 2006.

Reich-Ranicki, Marcel. "Geknebelt, geschulmeistert, verpaukert: Die Parabel vom Untergang des Intellektuellen. Der schwarze Humor eines Mannes aus Polen." In *Ein Patagonier in Berlin: Texte der deutschen Gombrowicz-Rezeption*. Edited by Marek Zybura, 45–48. Dresden: Neisse Verlag, 2018.

Ritz, German. "Körper, Geschlecht und Gender im autobiographischen Projekt Witold Gombrowiczs." In *Gombrowicz in Europa: Deutsch-polnische Versuche einer kulturellen Verortung*. Edited by Andreas Lawaty and Marek Zybura, 308–325. Wiesbaden: Harrassowitz, 2006.

Rodak, Paweł. "Dziennik Gombrowicza: Między mową, pismem i drukiem (wstępne rozpoznanie)." *Przegląd Filozoficzno-Literacki* 10, no. 4 (2001): 87–118.

Rosół, Piotr S. "Becoming Gombrowicz: On the Way of Trans-Subjectivity and Trans-Modernity." In *Gombrowicz in Transnational Context: Translation, Affect, and Politics*. Edited by Silvia G. Dapía, 115–125. New York: Routledge, 2019.

Sadzik, Piotr. "Listy Witolda Gombrowicza do Leo Lipskiego." *Teksty Drugie*, no. 6 (2020): 387–409.

Saer, Juan J. "La perspectiva exterior: Gombrowicz en la Argentina." In *El concepto de ficción*, 17–29. Los tres mundos Ensayo. Buenos Aires: Seix Barral, 2004.

Sandauer, Artur. "Witold Gombrowicz – człowiek i pisarz." In *Zebrane pisma krytyczne: Studia o literaturze współczesnej*. 3 vols., 581–613 1. Warszawa: Państwowy Instytut Wydawniczy, 1981.

Scholze, Dietrich. "Zum Auto-Image des polnischen Exils: Gombrowicz und Polen in *Dziennik* und *Trans-Atlantyk*." In *Gombrowicz in Europa: Deutsch-polnische*

Versuche einer kulturellen Verortung. Edited by Andreas Lawaty and Marek Zybura, 68–78. Wiesbaden: Harrassowitz, 2006.

Schulz, Bruno. "Ferdydurke." *Literary Studies in Poland* 10, no. 1983: 25–33.

Siedlecka, Joanna. "Gombrowicz w sieci bezpieki." Rzeczpospolita: Plus Minus, December 4, 2010. http://www.rp.pl/artykul/573405-Gombrowicz-w-sieci-bezpieki-.html&cid=44&template=restricted (accessed January 8, 2018).

Stowarzyszenia Miłość Nie Wyklucza. "Co o równości myślą Polacy i Polki: Wszystko o badaniach społecznych na temat równości małżeńskiej i akceptacji osób LGBT+.". https://mnw.org.pl/tematy/badania/ (accessed May 10, 2023).

Suchanow, Klementyna. "El Caso Gombrowicz: La Traduccion De Ferdydurke De 1947." *Hispamerica* 36, no. 107 (2007): 3–13.

Szczuka, Kazimiera. "Gombrowicz subwersywny." *Teksty drugie* 58, no. 5 (1999): 171–180.

Tatarkiewicz, Anna. "Anty-Wieszcz i jego prorok." *Więź*, VII–VIII (1972): 87–100.

Tomassucci, Giovana. "'I Owed a Great Deal to Them': Some Hypotheses About the Paradoxes of Jewish Assimilation in Gombrowicz's Works." *pl.it – rassegna italiana di argomenti polacchi*, no. 11 (2020): 102–118.

Warkocki, Błażej. "A Queer Construction of Identity in the *Memoir of Stefan Czarniecki* by Witold Gombrowicz." *Central Europe* 19, no. 1 (2021): 27–37.

Warkocki, Błażej. "What Really Happened Aboard the Banbury? Reading Gombrowicz with Eve Kosofsky Sedgwick." In *Gombrowicz in Transnational Context: Translation, Affect, and Politics*. Edited by Silvia G. Dapía, 126–141. New York: Routledge, 2019.

Wittlin, Józef. "Uwagi Wstępne." In *Trans-Atlantyk. Ślub: (Z wstępem Józefa Wittlina i komentarzem autora)*, 7–21. Paryż: Instytut Literacki, 1953.

Żołkoś, Monika. "Gombrowicz w świecie zwierząt." *Dialog* 651, no. 2 (2011): 137–143.

Other

Behemoth. "In the Absence Ov Light." In *The Satanist*. 2014. (Song)

Dobrzyński, Michał. *Operetka*. 2015. (Operetta)

Kolski, Jan J. *Pornografia*. 2003. (Film)

Skolimowski, Jerzy. *30 Door Key: Ferdydurke*. 1991. (Film)

Żuławski, Andrzej. *Cosmos*. 2015. (Film)

Illustration Information

Figure 1.1 Title: *Witold Gombrowicz in Vence*. Author: Bohdan Paczowski. Source: Krzysztof Dybciak (1981-07-10). "Wielkie doświadczenie literatury polskiej". *Tygodnik Solidarność* (15): 11. License: Public Domain. URL: https://pl.wikipedia.org/wiki/Witold_Gombrowicz#/media/Plik:Witold_Gombrowicz_by_Bohdan_Paczowski_-_detail.jpg. Access date: 19.05.2022.

Figure 2.1 Title: *Ulica Nowy Świat w Warszawie w dzień letni*. Date: 1892. Author: Władysław Podkowiński. Source: Muzeum Narodowe w Warszawie. License: Public Domain. URL: https://wolnelektury.pl/katalog/obraz/podkowinski-ulica-nowy-swiat-w-warszawie-w-dzien-letni/. Access date: 19.05.2022.

Figure 2.2 Title: *Straathoek in de Joodse wijk, met uithangborden in het Pools en Hebreeuws (Street Corner in the Jewish Quarter with signs in Polish and Hebrew)*. Author: Willem van de Poll. Date: 1934. Source: Van de Poll Photo Collection, Nationaal Archief (2.24.14.02, File Number: 190-0051). License: CC0. URL: https://commons.wikimedia.org/wiki/File:Straathoek_in_de_Joodse_wijk,_met_uithangborden_in_het_Pools_en_Hebreeuws,_Bestanddeelnr_190-0051.jpg#/media/File:Straathoek_in_de_Joodse_wijk,_met_uithangborden_in_het_Pools_en_Hebreeuws,_Bestanddeelnr_190-0051.jpg. Access date: 15.10.2023.

Figure 2.3 Title: *Dedykacja ("Dedication." Self Portrait in Cliché-Verre)*. Author: Bruno Schulz. Date: Between 1920 and 1922. Source: National Museum in Kraków License: Public Domain. URL: https://commons.wikimedia.org/wiki/File:Schulz_autoportet.jpg. Access date: 15.10.2023.

Figure 2.4 Title: *The Gombrowicz Mansion in Wsola*. Date: 2018. Author: Aleksandra Konarzewska.

Figure 3.1 Title: *Polish Passenger Ship MS Chrobry*. Date: 1939. Author: Unknown. Source: Witold J. Urbanowicz: *Transatlantyki: Zarys ich dziejów i techniki*, Wydawnictwo Morskie, Gdańsk 1977. License: Public Domain.

URL: https://commons.wikimedia.org/wiki/File:MS_ChrobryTrans.jpg. Access date: 15.10.2023.

Figure 3.2 Title: *A Yacimientos Petrolíferos Fiscales (YPF) gas station on the corner of Corrientes and Forest Avenues in Chacarita district of Buenos Aires, 1951. Inventory AGN 194863*. Date: 1951. Source: Archivo General de la Nación (AGN). Author: unknown. License: Public Domain. URL: https://upload.wikimedia.org/wikipedia/commons/f/f6/Buenos_Aires_-_Chacarita_-_Estaci%C3%B3n_de_servicio_YPF_1951.jpg. Access date: 19.05.2022.

Figure 3.3 Title: *Tango Between Men in Buenos Aires*. Author: Unknown. Date: No date. Source: Archivo General de la Nación. License: Public Domain. URL: https://commons.wikimedia.org/wiki/File:Tango-entre-homme.jpg. Access date: 15.10.2023.

Figure 3.4 Title: *German author Thomas Mann seated in a chair, Los Angeles*. Date: Between 1925 and 1945. Source: Los Angeles Daily News. License: CC BY 4.0 URL: https://commons.wikimedia.org/wiki/File:Thomas_Mann_in_Los_Angeles.jpg#/media/File:Thomas_Mann_in_Los_Angeles.jpg Access date: 15.10.2023.

Figure 4.1 Title: *Polish Hamlet—Portrait of Aleksander Wielopolski*. Author: Jacek Malczewski. Date: 1903. Source: Muzeum Narodowe w Warszawie. License: Public Domain. URL: https://commons.wikimedia.org/wiki/File:Jacek_Malczewski,_Hamlet_Polski_-_Portret_Aleksandra_Wielopolskiego.jpg. Access date: 15.10.2023.

Figure 4.2 Title: *Newspaper stand in Buenos Aires, by Grete Stern*. Date: 1956. Source: Buenos Aires Moderno, Ediciones Peuser, Buenos Aires, 1956. Author: Grete Stern. License: Public Domain. URL: https://upload.wikimedia.org/wikipedia/commons/6/69/Newspaper_stand_in_Buenos_Aires%2C_by_Grete_Stern.jpg. Access date: 19.05.2022.

Figure 4.3 Title: *Pejzaż morski*. Date: 1939. Author: Władysław Strzemiński. License: Public Domain. URL: https://commons.wikimedia.org/wiki/File:W%C5%82adys%C5%82aw_Strzemi%C5%84ski,_%22Pajza%C5%BC_morski%22.jpg. Access date: 15.10.2023.

Figure 5.1 Title: *Alfred Camus, Studio Photo*. Date: 1945. Source: RMN. Author: Studio Harcourt. License: Public Domain. URL: https://commons.wikimedia.org/wiki/File:Camus_Harcourt_1945.jpg. Access date: 15.10.2023.

Figure 5.2 Title: *Martin Buber in Palestine/Israel*. Author: Unknown. Date: Between 1940 and 1950. Source: The David B. Keidan Collection of Digital Images from the Central Zionist Archives (via Harvard University Library), License: Public Domain. URL: https://commons.wikimedia.org/wiki/Category:Martin_Buber#/media/File:Martin_Buber_portrait.jpg. Access date: 15.10.2023.

Figure 5.3 Title: *Władysław Gomułka addresses hundreds of thousand of people in Warsaw on 24 October 1956.* Date: 24 October 1956. Author: Unknown. License: Public Domain. URL: https://commons.wikimedia.org/wiki/File:Gomulka_speech.jpg. Access date: 15.10.2023.

Figure 5.4 Title: *Press Conference of Swedish Film Director Ingmar Bergman at the Amstel Hotel in Amsterdam.* Date: 10 October 1966. Author: Joost Evers/Anefo. License: Public Domain. URL: https://commons.wikimedia.org/wiki/File:Persconferenties,_filmregisseurs,_portretten,_Bergmann,_Ingmar,_Bestanddeelnr_919-6650.jpg. Access date: 15.10.2023.

Figure 5.5 Title: *Kurt Jacobsson and Christian Dior in 1957.* Date: 1957. Source: Digitalt museum, ID NMA.0097968 (cropped photograph of the cover of the staff newspaper of NK, Kompanirullan nr 3, 1957). Author: Unknown. License: Public Domain. URL: https://commons.wikimedia.org/wiki/File:Kurt_Jacobsson_and_Christian_Dior_1957.jpg. Access date: 15.10.2023.

Figure 6.1 Title: *Removal of Furniture in East Berlin near Bernauer Strasse, Early September 1961.* Date: 1961. Source: "A City Torn Apart: Building of the Berlin Wall." CIA's Historical Collections. Author: The Central Intelligence Agency. License: Public Domain. URL: https://commons.wikimedia.org/wiki/File:Removing_Furniture_in_East_Berlin_-_Flickr_-_The_Central_Intelligence_Agency.jpg. Access date: 15.10.2023.

Figure 6.2 Title: *Rock Refuge of Reverend Stolarczyk in the Tatra Mountains.* Date: 1876. Author: Walery Eljasz-Radzikowski. Source: National Museum Kraków. License: Public Domain. URL: https://commons.wikimedia.org/wiki/File:Walery_Eljasz-Radzikowski_-_Rock_Refuge_of_Reverend_Stolarczyk_in_the_Tatra_Mountains_-_MNK_II-a-684_-_National_Museum_Krak%C3%B3w.jpg. Access date: 15.10.2023.

Figure 6.3 Title: *Portrait Photograph of Arthur Schopenhauer.* Author: Schäfer, J. Date: 1859. Source: Frankfurt am Main University Library. License: Public Domain. URL: https://commons.wikimedia.org/wiki/File:Arthur_Schopenhauer_by_J_Sch%C3%A4fer,_1859_(cropped).jpg#/media/File:Arthur_Schopenhauer_by_J_Sch%C3%A4fer,_1859_(cropped).jpg. Access date: 15.10.2023.

Name Index

Subject Index

For Product Safety Concerns and Information please contact our EU representative GPSR@taylorandfrancis.com
Taylor & Francis Verlag GmbH, Kaufingerstraße 24, 80331 München, Germany

www.ingramcontent.com/pod-product-compliance
Lightning Source LLC
LaVergne TN
LVHW010932110826
845149LV00013B/2564

* 9 7 8 1 0 3 2 0 2 5 7 5 9 *